# Shifting Fortunes

# SHIFTING FORTUNES

---

*The Rise and Decline of American
Labor, from the 1820s to the Present*

---

## Daniel Nelson

*The American Ways Series*

IVAN R. DEE    *Chicago*

Library of Congress Cataloging-in-Publication Data:
Nelson, Daniel, 1941–
    Shifting fortunes : the rise and decline of American labor, from the 1820s to the present / Daniel Nelson.
        p.   cm.  — (American ways series)
    Includes bibliographical references and index.
    ISBN 1-56663-179-3 (cloth : alk. paper). —
ISBN 1-56663-180-7  (pbk. : alk. paper)
        1. Labor—United States—History.   2. Labor movement—United States—History.   3. Trade-unions—United States—History.   4. Industrial relations—United States—History.
I. Title.  II. Series.
HD8066.N37  1997
331'.0973—DC21                                        97-22108

*To Lorraine*

# Contents

# Preface

MOST HISTORIES of the American labor movement emphasize ideology or union structure and assume that they explain the ability of unions to recruit members. This book focuses on union growth itself and argues that external factors, notably employer policies and government actions, have been as important, if not more important, in explaining the growth of organized labor in the United States.

Wage earners historically have sought a formal voice in determining the circumstances of their work. Unions have been the most prominent and clearest expression of that desire. At any given time the level of union membership is thus a measure of the workers' success in translating their desire for voice into a particular institutional form. If workers' desires were constant and conclusive, union membership would also be reasonably constant and probably considerably higher than it was and is. The relatively low level and fluctuating character of union membership suggests that other influences, apart from the desire for voice, had and have an important, often decisive impact.

My principal concern, however, is not *why* unions grew but *how* they grew. I have tried to view union activity as it happened, as a sequence of events over time. A historical approach emphasizes the dynamism of organized labor and the danger of generalizations based on examining brief periods or limited experience.

There is no shortage of historical works on American labor history. Indeed, the literature is rich and illuminating, and I have drawn on it extensively, as the Note on Sources indicates. But this is not a summary of other people's books. It is an effort to make sense of union activity over time and to provide a useful introduction to a fascinating, controversial topic.

# Shifting Fortunes

# 1

# Union Growth in Perspective

FOR MORE THAN a century and a half, wage earners have sought to improve their jobs and their lives by creating or joining unions. Their efforts have enjoyed varying degrees of success. The record of those efforts is probably the most revealing guide to the character of working-class life in the United States. It is also an invaluable source of information on related issues such as the impact of technological change and political protest movements. The *reasons* for the ever-changing number of American union members are more elusive. Internal factors—the character of the members and leaders, for example—obviously matter. But external influences, such as employer policies, have also been extremely influential. The challenge is to identify those factors that explain union activity over time.

The following table summarizes the best available data on union density (union members as a percentage of the nonagricultural wage-earning labor force) between the 1820s and the present. Although the numbers reflect as much guesswork as actual counting, they probably capture the relative differences between periods. Union membership seemingly followed an irregular pattern of expansion and decline, with each peak higher than the previous one and each trough the same or slightly higher—until the 1970s, when a period of steady decline began. What accounted for these marked differences? The difficulty of explaining what happened is apparent from a brief examination of two recurring themes, the role of union leadership and the impact of the American economic and political environment.

ESTIMATES OF UNION DENSITY, 1820s–1990s
(percentage of nonagricultural labor force)

|            | High         | Low          |
|------------|--------------|--------------|
| 1820s–1840s | 2–3 (1836)   | NA           |
| 1850s–1870s | 5 (1873)     | NA           |
| 1870s–1890s | 6 (1886)     | 3.5 (1897)   |
| 1900–1915  | 12.3 (1904)  | 6.1 (1900)   |
| 1915–1922  | 19.6 (1921)  | 11.2 (1916)  |
| 1923–1932  | 12.8 (1923)  | 10.7 (1930)  |
| 1933–1945  | 35.5 (1945)  | 11.3 (1933)  |
| 1946–1979  | 34.7 (1954)  | 23.6 (1978)  |
| 1980–1994  | 22.7 (1980)  | 15.5 (1994)  |

To attribute membership fluctuations to the activities of specific individuals is tempting and logical. It personalizes complex processes and emphasizes the obvious: the leadership of William Sylvis, Terence V. Powderly, Samuel Gompers, John L. Lewis, Walter Reuther, or George Meany unquestionably made a difference, as did the work of thousands of lesser-known individuals. If it made a *crucial* difference, explaining the ups and downs in union membership would be easy. But that was rarely, if ever, the case. Consider two famous examples. Critics of the American Federation of Labor (and, alas, many later historians) often equated President Samuel Gompers with the AFL, as if his ideas and biases were the ideas and biases of all union members and leaders, and dictated the fate of the labor movement. Yet even the most cursory examination of the events of Gompers's career shows that his ideas bound no one and in fact were rejected by many loyal and enthusiastic union members. Gompers was not the labor movement, or even a particularly helpful symbol of the labor movement.

Later critics condemned his successor, William Green, as a weak and ineffectual leader with little or no weight. Yet Green presided over the most sustained expansion of union influence in American history. Gompers and Green held the same position, had almost identical formal powers, and relied on the same groups of supporters. Could their contributions have been so different? Obviously much more was involved than the leadership of these men. Although quality of leadership mattered, it explains only a fraction of the changes in union density.

The temptation to emphasize individual leadership is particularly dangerous in the case of the labor movement, which has been and remains highly decentralized. National unions, the basic unit since the late nineteenth century, are largely autonomous, and local (and in some cases regional) organizations also have substantial powers. These organizations have vastly different internal structures and policies toward employers and government. Leaders of national union federations such as the AFL and the Congress of Industrial Organizations (CIO) had to win the cooperation of these bodies in order to influence them. Many times they succeeded, often they failed. But if organizational autonomy meant that unions could go their own way, it also allowed many opportunities for individual achievement. Because of these opportunities, the labor movement rarely suffered a dearth of promising leaders.

To take the opposite tack and emphasize the decisive effect of economic or political conditions on individual or group behavior is equally dangerous. In its most extreme form, this approach reduces the individual to a cipher, wholly at the mercy of impersonal forces. Even in more reasonable forms, such an approach can be misleading. A prime example is the work of the economist John R. Commons and his students (notably Selig Perlman), among the first and most influential interpreters of the American labor movement. Commons's interest in economic theories based on real-life experiences led to his pioneering, collaborative study, *History of Labour in the United States* (4 volumes, 1918–1935). Although the books are relentlessly empirical, Commons and his students, principally Perlman, could not resist the temptation to draw conclusions from their data. While the *History of Labour* is a treasure trove of valuable information, it is best known for a few pages of analysis which are only tangentially related to the narrative.

In essence the Commons group argued that American workers, responding to a distinctive economic and political environment, became "wage conscious" rather than class conscious, and created a craft-oriented (based on identifiable, usually skilled occupations), politically conservative labor movement that reflected American conditions. Intellectuals tried repeatedly to make American workers class conscious and anticapitalist, only to fail with equal frequency. Eventually workers themselves adopted a more logical and pragmatic approach to organization, embodied in the American Federation of Labor. So-called business unionism, devoted to improving wages and working conditions for mostly skilled union members, was thus an inevitable outgrowth of American conditions. Men such as Gompers and Green did not shape the labor movement; they simply recognized the limitations of their environment and refused to waste time tilting at windmills. The Commons interpretation seemed to explain the state of the labor movement in the 1920s, when most of their interpretive material was published.

In recent years Commons and his students have come under steady attack. In the first place they provided no evidence of a distinctive "wage consciousness." By definition, all wage earners are wage conscious, but there is no reason to believe that American wage earners (most of whom until the 1930s were European immigrants or children of immigrants) were more wage conscious than their friends and relatives back home, or that such a viewpoint, if it existed, precluded class sensitivities. In fact, recent studies of nineteenth-century American industrial workers have detected a high degree of class consciousness—hardly a surprise, given the huge disparities in wealth and power between industrial workers and their employers.

The rest of the Commons theory has fared no better. The attack on intellectuals was no better grounded than the notion of wage consciousness. Writers, scholars, and agitators made important contributions to union growth and vitality in the nineteenth and twentieth centuries. Their more politically oriented unionism competed effectively with business unionism. The result of this widely varied activity was an American labor movement similar in size and breadth to European labor movements until the early twentieth century, and again in the years after World War II. The point is not to pillory Commons and his students but to illustrate the problems that result from an excessive emphasis on American "conditions."

The chapters in this book examine the experiences of American workers over a century and a half of union activity. They do not advance an overarching theory or even suggest that such a theory is possible. They do, however, emphasize three factors that help to explain the fluctuations in union density documented in the table above: (1) the role of autonomous workers (that is, workers who exercise a high degree of influence over what they do and how they do it); (2) the impact of reprisals or the threat of reprisals on the willingness of individuals to join or remain in a union; and (3) the economic and political environment.

### ONE: WORKER AUTONOMY

Some kinds of jobs are more conducive to a collective voice (other things being equal) than others. This may seem obvious, but specifying the kinds of jobs that are or are not conducive to organization is more difficult. It leads to misconceptions about unions and union members. For example, a common and seemingly commonsense assertion is that industrial or "blue-collar" occupations are most organizable. Unions have long been associated with blue-collar jobs (construction or factory work, for example), but perhaps only because the number of workers in those occupations were growing rapidly in the late nineteenth and early twentieth centuries when organized labor became a powerful force in the economy. Any important labor force development at that time was likely to involve construction or factory workers. In fact, only a fraction of blue-collar workers were union members at any given time. Since the 1960s most new workers have been "white collar" rather than blue collar, and the number of white-collar union members has grown rapidly and will likely continue to grow, reflecting this trend.

Another common and potentially misleading suggestion is that "skilled" (implicitly skilled blue-collar) workers were most likely to organize. There is some truth to this statement too, but so many exceptions that its value is questionable. Many workers with hard-to-find skills have formed powerful unions. Railroad operating employees are prime examples, as are tool and die makers, plumbers, and many others. But most highly skilled workers (such as engineers, scientists, and, more recently, medical professionals) have not been union members. In addition, the stock of skilled jobs has evolved more rapidly than the unions that have purported to represent them, further confusing the issue. And perhaps most perplexing, the majority of union members at most times have been less-skilled workers. The largest and most important union during the first half of the twentieth century was the United Mine Workers, composed mainly of low-skill employees.

A more useful concept than either "blue collar" or "skill" is workplace autonomy. Workers who were most likely to organize, organize successfully, and spearhead the organization of other, less fortunate workers were those who worked with little direct supervision, who planned and executed their work on the basis of technical knowledge, experience, and common sense. Although they were wage earners, they enjoyed substantial personal freedom in the workplace. Examples include all of the skilled jobs noted above as well as miners, construction workers, and many service employees.

What was the connection between workplace autonomy and organization? Any answer must account for the diverse circumstances and economic conditions that also influenced workers' behavior, but two factors were critical. First, workplace autonomy meant that workers had greater physical freedom to interact with coworkers, to discuss problems and interests and act in concert. The nature of their work created opportunities for collaborative activity that more regimented employees did not share. The people they were most likely to interact with were those who had similar jobs. Workplace autonomy naturally led to craft or job-specific organization.

Second, workplace autonomy had an important psychological effect. Autonomous workers were more likely to identify with their jobs, to develop a sense of "ownership." By most measures, coal mining was one of the least desirable occupations. Yet coal miners were notorious for their attachment to the industry and to the labor movement. Like other autonomous workers, they sought to preserve the character of the job while relying on unions to improve wages and working conditions.

Workplace autonomy also helps explain what did *not* happen—in particular, the poor record of union organization among factory workers. The failure of the labor movement to attract large numbers of factory workers before the 1930s provoked endless debate. Pro-union commentators pointed to it as proof of union incompetence and employer perfidy; opponents cited it as evidence of the un-American character of the labor movement. But another dimension of the issue received less attention. Because of the character of their work, factory workers had less opportunity to unionize. With few exceptions they had less autonomy than miners, construction workers, and service employees. Except for highly expendable laborers, they were machine operators, subject to the directions of powerful, ever-present supervisors. Intrusive management limited both the workers' physical freedom and their sense of job ownership.

Many wage earners in manufacturing did organize, but their experiences only emphasized the constraints on factory employees. Most of those who succeeded in forming and sustaining unions before the 1930s were employed in primitive factories, such as cigar-making or clothing plants. Although they often bemoaned their lowly status relative to the classic artisan, they retained considerable influence on the character of the work environment and the level of production. Unions translated this influence into economic power. Factory employees in labor-intensive manufacturing industries such as shoes, pottery, and stove-making also formed powerful unions. But employees in capital-intensive and especially in mass-production industries, the industries that have dominated twentieth-century manufacturing, were less successful. With few exceptions they formed durable unions only when they received outside support, usually in the form of government assistance.

### Two: Reprisals

Regardless of occupation or industry, union membership will grow only when workers are convinced that the benefits of membership outweigh the potential costs. Many workers who favor a collective voice when the cost is low become less enthusiastic as the prospect of reprisals, especially discharges or plant closings, grows. A few workers are committed; the majority, however, are pragmatists: their behavior depends on the likely result. What does the union offer? How will the employer react? Above all, will membership lead to discharge or other forms of punishment?

Union leaders and employers try to circumvent or exploit such concerns. Unions typically seek union security agreements that require membership as a condition of employment (a "closed shop") and seemingly eliminate the possibility of reprisals. Employers favor "open-shop" policies that exclude unions from the workplace and raise the expectation of reprisals. But there are many ways to influence workers' decisions that stop well short of the closed or open shop. Unions provide a range of social and cultural opportunities and serve as advocates for political causes. They also provide a sense of group solidarity that may otherwise not exist for many workers. Conversely, employers adopt personnel policies that diminish the appeal of such services. Welfare programs, common to big business and some small businesses since the late nineteenth century, have many objectives, such as improving productivity and reducing labor turnover. By increasing the attractiveness of the job, they also tend to reduce the appeal of unions.

Unions face an additional hurdle because aggrieved workers can simply leave—that is, find another job with more desirable qualities. As long as jobs are available, some workers will choose exit over voice. In these situations, labor turnover may be an alternative to union membership. Whether it is usually depends on other factors such as the policies of employers and government. Another, very different option is to force employers to provide certain minimum conditions or benefits through political action. This usually requires a high degree of organization, whether or not unions are involved.

## THREE: THE ORGANIZING ENVIRONMENT

Environmental factors strongly influence workers' assessments of their options at any given time. Three are crucial: the overall performance of the economy (level of production, income, unemployment, inflation, and so on), the extent and effectiveness of economic regulation, and the employer's business goals.

Good times and inflation are usually conducive to union growth; recessions and deflation typically discourage growth, regardless of other factors. Nineteenth-century union growth and decline were highly correlated with business cycles and price movements. The 1930s provide other well-documented examples. The Great Depression of 1929–1932 led to the virtual collapse of the labor movement. Recovery, from 1933 to 1937, coincided with union revival. The recession of 1937–1938 saw renewed decline, and the recovery that began in 1938 was accompanied by vigorous union growth.

Government regulation is also influential. Government-mandated collective bargaining during World War I encouraged union growth. The Wagner Act, which encouraged collective bargaining and became effective in mid-1937, stimulated membership growth, and the War Labor Board's maintenance-of-membership policies in World War II had an even greater positive effect. Other forms of industrial regulation reinforced these trends. The most highly organized industries of the middle decades of the twentieth century were regulated industries such as transportation.

Employers' business goals also have a substantial impact on union prospects. Nearly all employers oppose unions in principle, yet a large majority of them were and are pragmatists. They calculate the economic effects of policy options and adjust principles to economic reality. Employers who decide that a strike will have a disastrous effect are more amenable to worker demands than those who feel immune because they have other plants, large inventories, or poor prospects (in a recession period, for example). In the preregulation era, the small minority of firms that bargained with unions almost all operated single plants, relied on labor-intensive production methods, and operated in highly competitive industries.

Who were America's union members? By and large they were workers who enjoyed a high degree of workplace freedom, who believed that the benefits of union membership outweighed the costs, and who were sensitive to changing economic and political conditions. Their numbers varied from year to year, as the table indicates. The fluctuations were

partly the result of workers dropping in or out as short-term
conditions changed, but also of longer-term shifts between industries and jobs, as economic and political events foreclosed
opportunities for some workers and created them for others.

# 2

# Miners and Organized Labor

THE TRANSFORMATION of the economy in the mid-nineteenth century created two distinct organizational paths that shaped the American labor movement for more than a century. The first, examined in this chapter, originated in the countryside, in the most challenging and dangerous work of that era. Miners of coal, copper, gold, silver, and other minerals produced the raw materials essential to an industrial economy. Their work, however, consisted of simple hand tasks planned and executed at the job site and performed alone or in conjunction with a handful of other workers. Together with the mine environment and the isolated setting typical of most mines, the character of their work made miners the most insistent advocates of formal organization. Andrew Roy, a prominent figure in the coal industry, recalled that "neither persuasion nor discharge could induce [miners] to renounce allegiance to the principle of combination." The same factors influenced their unions. Miners paid little attention to differences between jobs or individual workers and emphasized collective, mass action in confronting employers.

PERSPECTIVE: 1894

The depression of the 1890s, the most severe of the century, devastated unions generally, but none more than the United Mine Workers, the national union of coal miners. An 1890 amalgam of state organizations and Knights of Labor assemblies, the UMW was one of the largest American unions. It had agreements with employers in many fields; its president, John McBride, was arguably the most prominent labor leader. Yet it was untested. In previous depressions miners' unions, like most unions, had collapsed. Would the larger UMW have a different fate? Its destiny would be a measure of the organization McBride and other union leaders had created.

By the spring of 1894 the decline of raw materials prices had severely affected the mining industries and provoked widespread wage cutting. In the Pennsylvania and Midwestern bituminous coal fields, the slump threatened to destroy the workplace order and stability that had seemed within reach a year or two before. McBride and the UMW executive council resolved on a bold move: a national strike that would curtail production until prices rose and eventually raise the miners' wages. The strike was set for April 21. McBride predicted that 132,000 miners would participate and hinted that the total might reach 300,000 if the anthracite miners of northeastern Pennsylvania joined the strike. The actual number of strikers is impossible to calculate, though McBride claimed that about 80,000 workers heeded the initial strike call. Others joined the strike after May 1, when their wage agreements expired, and many thousands left their jobs for fear of the strikers' wrath. Perhaps 165,000 workers in every mining state between Pennsylvania and Kansas were voluntary or involuntary participants—90 percent of all bituminous miners and more than half of all coal miners. For a union with a paid-up membership of 20,000 on the eve of the conflict, the strike was an impressive demonstration of union influence.

McBride and other UMW executives coordinated strike activities from the union's national office in Columbus, Ohio, and from the several state headquarters, but they did not direct the strike in any important sense. The union had no strike fund, virtually no treasury, and no authority over individual locals. Each local (or in the case of nonmember participants, each mine or group of mines) voted to join or not join the strike, and later to accept or not accept the strike settlement. The UMW, like most unions, was more a confederation of locals than a unitary organization. In 1894 union activism meant local activism.

The success of the strike depended on the cessation of mining, so that shortages would force up prices and make employers willing to raise wages. In some fields the union used organizers to enlist nonstriking miners. By mid-May the UMW had a half-dozen organizers in southern West Virginia, the least organized of the major bituminous fields. Ominously, a mob of eastern European immigrants murdered one of them. The others survived but accomplished little. Anti-union employers persuaded their black employees, a large minority of the total, that they, not the union, could best protect the workers' interests.

In other areas where union and nonunion mines were intermixed, organized workers spread the strike themselves. Their preferred technique was the mass march or "raid." Strikers would march or parade to the target establishment, gather at the entrances, and harangue and harass nonstrikers until they joined the strike. Union leaders insisted that their goal was to "persuade" workers to join the strike, but the mass march, by its very nature, was intimidating and coercive. If the employer responded to the strikers' challenge, either by hiring guards or enlisting the local sheriff and his deputies, the likelihood of violence increased. Approximately a dozen people died during the 1894 strike, mostly as a result of mass marches.

On April 26 strikers from Spring Valley, La Salle, Peru, and Streator, all northern Illinois mining towns, marched on Toluca, a nonunion town operated by the Devlin Coal Mining Company. More than 3,500 armed miners joined the march, accompanied by wagons loaded with food and beer. By 5 a.m. on April 27 the strikers had gathered outside Toluca, terrifying the town's residents, including its 500 miners. The sheriff hurriedly recruited 50 deputies and called for the National Guard. Instead the governor and the UMW district officers rushed to Toluca. At sunrise the footsore marchers paraded into town, four abreast, preceded by brass bands, a fife-and-drum corps, and a small orchestra. After brief speeches, the marchers adjourned to the saloons to await their leaders' instructions. Later that morning union officers and the governor addressed a mass meeting and conferred with the mine owner. By noon the crisis had ended. Although the operator remained intransigent, UMW officials assured the strikers that they would prevail. The governor arranged for a free train to take the marchers back to their homes. Several days later the Toluca miners voted to join the strike.

Mass marches closed many mines in Illinois and Indiana, where there were initially many holdouts. But as the strike continued and the strikers became more impatient, disciplined mass action gradually gave way to mob activity. Strikers destroyed mine property and confronted deputies and soldiers. A gun battle between strikers and deputies in La Salle, Illinois, in late May, symbolized the increasingly violent and desperate character of the marches. In several cases be-

sieging strikers formed semipermanent encampments outside
hostile communities. The specter of civil war haunted the region. By late May the National Guard patrolled coal towns in
Maryland, Pennsylvania, Ohio, Indiana, West Virginia, Illinois, and Iowa.

The strikers' failure to close the southern West Virginia
fields led to a second type of militant action. After mid-May
the strikers increasingly directed their wrath against the railroads that transported West Virginia coal to Northern and
Eastern cities. Mobs halted trains at stations and forced crews
to move coal cars to sidings. In some cases strikers comman-
deered entire trains; in others they derailed or overturned
cars. At Knightsville, Indiana, a mob attacked a train, killing
the engineer. By June soldiers accompanied all trains between
Bellaire, Ohio, on the West Virginia border, and Cambridge,
Ohio, on the northern edge of the mining region. As service
improved, strikers retaliated by destroying bridges and tres-
tles. Union leaders enlisted the aid of the American Railway
Union, then at the peak of its influence, but received no help
from the powerful Brotherhood of Locomotive Engineers.
Coal shipments continued. The strikers' attacks forced local
and state officials, many of whom were prolabor, to oppose the
strike.

Meanwhile UMW leaders sought a collective bargaining
agreement embracing the entire industry. For more than a
month McBride and his executive council refused to negotiate
with individual coal operators. In mid-May they scheduled a
negotiating conference in Cleveland which attracted more
than a hundred operators. Yet the conference failed because
many important employers did not attend and those who did
were unwilling to raise wages to a level that would satisfy the
strikers. Other abortive conferences followed. Finally, with

the strike on the verge of collapse, a group of Pennsylvania and Midwestern owners hammered out an agreement with McBride and UMW leaders.

The new wage scale was only marginally higher and did not include the southern West Virginia fields. Many strikers were shocked. Nearly every rank-and-file gathering initially rejected the pact, and the Ohio district president mounted a secession movement from the national union. McBride, however, ultimately prevailed. He argued that the union was bankrupt, many of its local and district officers imprisoned, and the strike near collapse. "We had reached the dangerline and made the best we could of the situation," he explained. Reluctantly the workers agreed. By late June 1894 most of them had returned to work.

What had this conflict—the greatest union-inspired American strike to that time—accomplished? Initially very little. The depression continued for two more years, eroding the 1894 agreement and the idea of union-imposed stability. Although McBride defeated Samuel Gompers for the AFL presidency in September 1894, he served a fitful term, grew discouraged, and turned to third-party politics and populism. The economic recovery of the late 1890s demonstrated that the strike had been a better idea. The UMW soon became the largest and most influential American union. The 1894 strike proved to be a dress rehearsal for more durable victories in 1897, 1900, 1902, and later.

But two other features of the strike may have been more significant. In 1894 the strikers' tactics had been as notable as their objectives. With virtually no resources they had effectively paralyzed a major industry for a month, demonstrating—as miners had for half a century—the power of a broad-based, united workers' movement. At the same time their failures south of the Ohio compromised their Northern successes and exposed their vulnerability. As the UMW consolidated its position in the Northern fields, the still unorganized Southern fields became a greater and greater threat to union goals.

## MINERS AND MINING

Mining as a distinctive industry was largely nonexistent before the 1820s and became a notable employer of industrial workers only in the 1840s. The earliest mines appeared where outcroppings of coal, iron ore, or other minerals made extraction comparatively simple. In western Maryland, for example, Irish laborers who had been employed in the building of the Chesapeake and Ohio Canal found a ready market for their labor in the region's primitive open-pit coal mines. As demand for coal and other minerals burgeoned, employment rose (ninefold between 1830 and 1860), and underground mining prevailed. Although large-scale open-pit mining later became common in iron and copper mining, it was the underground mine and the underground miner that defined the labor movement and accounted for the industry's fractious labor-management relations.

The underground mine was a product of centuries of European and South American experience and local adaptation to geological conditions. Miners dug tunnels into the sides of mountains or vertical shafts into the ground. Tunnels extended from the shafts, typically at multiple levels; individual work rooms (called "breasts" in anthracite mining and "stopes" in copper, gold, and silver mining) opened off the tunnels. The mine was also a marvel of mechanical creativity. Its steam engine powered elevators, operated pumps, and drove the air compressors that supplied power to cutting machines, drills, and other machinery. In anthracite mining, huge above-ground breakers broke the coal into salable pieces. In gold, silver, and copper mining, mills and smelters often overshadowed the mines themselves.

All this activity depended on the individual miner who initiated and controlled the process of coal or ore extraction. The miner's primary function was to drill the mine face, pack the holes with explosives, and blast the ore and rock into usable pieces. In bituminous mines, where miners usually worked alone, they undercut the coal face with a pick, drilled holes, and shoveled the broken coal into cars. In anthracite and hard-rock mines, where drilling was more difficult and time consuming, they typically worked in teams and did little or no shoveling. Miners tried to work at an upward angle so that the loosened rock would fall back toward the entrance of the room. In hard-rock mines one man would hold the drill while the other wielded a sledgehammer. In the 1880s the introduction of undercutting machines and pneumatic drills made the miner's job less arduous but more unhealthy because of the clouds of dust they created. Otherwise the drills did not change the character of mining or reduce the miner's autonomy.

Except in small bituminous mines, miners were typically a minority of the mine labor force. The exact ratio of miners to other workers depended on the extent of the above-ground operation. In anthracite mining more than one-third of all employees were above ground; in gold mining the proportion was often closer to two-thirds. Below ground, miners worked alongside laborers (coal miners often employed their own laborers; hard-rock miners relied on company men), mule drivers, trappers (boys who operated the ventilation system), and mechanics. Except for carpenters, blacksmiths, and other skilled mechanical workers, these employees earned less than miners and were considered inferior to them. Drivers, trappers, and breaker boys were usually apprentice miners; muckers and trammers, who loaded and moved cars in copper mines, were simply laborers. Tensions between miners and other mine employees could be a deterrent to collective activity. In Michigan copper mines, for example, friction between miners and trammers discouraged union activity. In Butte, Montana, conflicts between miners and other employees ultimately led to the destruction of the Butte Miners Union, the most formidable of the Western miners' locals. Yet these were exceptional cases. Powerful unifying forces offset the divisions between miners and other mine employees.

One of these was the relatively unskilled character of mining. Miners' skills were typically acquired through observation and on-the-job training. As a prominent engineer noted, "Ordinary 'laboring men' under experienced supervision can be trained to become efficient miners in a short time." Beyond that minimum, skill had little economic value; indeed, veteran miners might produce less because of their sensitivity to mine hazards. West Virginia mines were highly productive despite their reliance on inexperienced workers. They were also notable for their astronomical accident rates.

The mine's physical environment also contributed to the cohesiveness of the labor force. Mining was by far the most dangerous occupation: casualty rates in some fields were comparable to those of armies in combat. Most deaths resulted from roof cave-ins and other small-scale disasters, but explosions, fires, and floods added materially to the toll. Miners fortunate enough to avoid accidents often suffered from miners' consumption or other respiratory afflictions that shortened careers and contributed to premature deaths.

In addition to such hazards, the darkness of the pre-1920 mine distinguished it from other workplaces. Until the introduction of electric power, miners depended on candles or oil lamps. It was only practical to illuminate the immediate work site, usually with a single candle or lamp. One of the most formidable challenges for new workers was to learn to work in almost complete darkness.

These conditions meant that intrusive supervision was impossible. Miners worked under contract or piece-rate systems that paid them for their output; otherwise they were largely free of managerial constraints. They worked at their own pace and left when they finished their work, regardless of the time. Few industrial jobs offered a comparable degree of autonomy. As long as miners retained the support of the laborers who worked with them, they had almost complete control of the workplace.

These features of mining created special challenges for mine owners and managers. A new mine required as much machinery as a small factory, but the machinery did not produce coal, copper, or precious metals; it simply enabled the miners and other employees to do their jobs. Additional investment could improve above-ground activities but not the miner's productivity. Any attempt to speed up mining risked more accidents. Barring a technological breakthrough, geology and the labor-intensive mining process were major obstacles to innovation.

Formidable external challenges reinforced the operator's sense of helplessness. As coal mining spread through northern Appalachia and into Indiana and Illinois, a competitive market emerged. Prices reflected demand and supply, notably seasonal demand (high in the fall, low in the spring and summer), and various unpredictable factors. No mine or mining company was big enough or innovative enough to affect the market. Profits were low, and most coal companies were short-lived. Ninety-five percent of anthracite coal companies in Schuylkill County, Pennsylvania, failed in the last quarter of the nineteenth century. Other operators were more fortunate. Gold and silver producers benefited from government subsidies. Michigan copper companies dominated the market until the 1890s and earned high profits. Thereafter a handful of powerful newcomers, notably the Guggenheims and Rockefellers, created an oligopoly that sustained the copper producers' profits.

Because of the critical role of labor in mining and the workers' cohesiveness, operators had little choice but to take their workers seriously. Like most employers, they sought ways to reduce labor costs. They cut wages when demand slackened and charged exorbitant prices for company housing and store goods. They also encouraged ethnic succession, replacing old stock or British workers with "new" immigrant workers (or black and Mexican workers in southern Appalachia and the Southwest, respectively). By 1900 old-stock miners had virtually disappeared, except in Alaska, and most Cornish, Welsh, English, and German miners held supervisory positions. The northern Michigan mining towns were as cosmopolitan as any major city. Even Butte, the most heavily Irish community in late-nineteenth-century America, began to experience the tensions and conflicts characteristic of more diverse cities.

Apart from such efforts, some employers developed two other labor strategies. The first, common in copper and gold mining, was to win the workers' goodwill by improving conditions outside the workplace. Leading exponents of welfare work included Calumet & Hecla, the largest of the Michigan copper companies; Homestake Mining of Lead, South Dakota, and Treadwell Mining of Douglas, Alaska, the largest American gold mining companies; and Colorado Fuel & Iron, the leading Western coal company. They provided good quality, low-cost housing and other community services that made their camps superior to most mining towns. Phoebe

Hearst, the philanthropic owner of Homestake, was the most famous of the paternalistic operators. Hearst and others argued that such expenditures made economic sense by reducing turnover and inspiring loyalty. They also discouraged union activity. Calumet & Hecla and Treadwell kept unions at bay for many years. Homestake employees formed one of the largest and most durable miners' unions, the Lead City Miners Union, but it was, in the words of the company's historian, "charitable, non-aggressive, and conservative." Union and company officials informally resolved grievances and coordinated company-sponsored beneficial activities. The Lead City union never struck.

The second, seemingly contradictory approach of some employers was to cooperate with workers and their representatives through collective bargaining. Formal collective bargaining was more common in coal mining than in any other industry. Small firm size, intense price competition, and high employee turnover encouraged efforts to contain market forces. Employers favored collective bargaining when the union had enough members to join them in a cartel; because of the labor-intensive character of production, stabilizing labor costs stabilized the industry. The resulting agreements aimed at reducing competition between firms by eliminating interfield wage differentials. Until the rise of the United Mine Workers, however, periods of harmony alternated with periods of competition, turmoil, and conflict, as the workers' demand for a collective voice clashed with the operators' struggle for profitability.

## MINERS' UNIONS, 1850–1894

The growth of the mining industries was a powerful stimulus to organization and union activity. Difficult and dangerous working conditions, a high degree of worker autonomy, irregular operations, and competitive markets were conducive to exit *and* voice. Miners changed jobs frequently in a never-ending search for steady work, better conditions, and higher wages. But they also organized on the job to preserve what they had already won or to achieve new objectives. Unlike many industries, where the collapse of a strike was followed by years of passivity, miners often reorganized within months. One reason was their mobility: strikers or former strikers moved on to new jobs, and other men, who had not participated in the strike but shared the strikers' perspectives, took their places. Despite the high rate of ethnic succession, the pattern did not vary. Indeed, the issue was not whether miners would opt for a collective voice but how and when they would create effective industry-wide unions. The process of organization-building occurred in two stages. The period to the mid-1890s was one of experimentation; the years from the mid-1890s to the 1920s brought fulfillment for coal miners and disaster for hard-rock miners.

The process of experimentation dated from 1849, when miners in Schuylkill County, Pennsylvania, created the "Bates" union, the first regional organization of coal miners. John Bates, an English political reformer, was the principal organizer and leader of the union, which conducted strikes and public demonstrations against low wages and company store abuses. The Bates union succumbed to internal divisions after a few months. The following year western Maryland bituminous miners won a six-week strike by enlisting the services of a former Scottish miners' union official as organizer. Other short-lived unions appeared in both anthracite and bituminous fields in the 1850s, but no effort rose above these ad hoc arrangements until 1861, when southern Illinois miners organized the American Miners Association, the first national miners' union. The Association spread to northern Illinois and, after several successful strikes, to the Tuscarawas, Mahoning, and Hocking valleys of Ohio, the Blossburg area of central Pennsylvania, the Monongahela Valley of southwestern Pennsylvania, western Maryland, and the Pittsburgh area. A journal, the *Weekly Miner*, provided cohesion.

A critical event in the history of the Association and, indirectly, in the history of miners' unions, occurred in early 1865, when the Blossburg operators locked out their employees in an effort to destroy the union. The conflict began when the union rejected an employer demand for housing leases that permitted immediate evictions, contrary to Pennsylvania law. After several months of idleness, the operators used their political power to obtain legislation providing for evictions after ten days' notice in company towns. The sheriff, with the assistance of troops, carried out the evictions. Four thousand residents, together with their possessions, were loaded onto trains and taken under guard to Blossburg, where they were unceremoniously dumped. Many union leaders were arrested. They and others, blacklisted, moved to other fields. Fifty years later Andrew Roy could report that they or their descendants "can be found in every mining region of the country." The miners who remained at Blossburg returned to work under "ironclad" nonunion contracts at lower wages.

No lives were lost, but the Blossburg conflict foreshadowed the battles of the following decades. The roles of sheriffs and troops, evictions and deportations, all became characteristic of miners' disputes. The lockout also marked the beginning of harder times for the American Miners Association. The end of the Civil War meant the end of wartime labor shortages and inflation, which had encouraged organization. Employers demanded wage reductions and had little trouble recruiting strikebreakers. By 1867 the Association had collapsed.

For the next decade two parallel developments shaped mine unionism. The discovery of the spectacular Comstock Lode, a virtual mountain of silver, and the growth of miners' communities at Gold Hill and Virginia City, Nevada, left an indelible imprint on the Western labor movement. The rapid expansion of anthracite mining in northeastern Pennsylvania had a similar impact in the East. By the mid-1870s the link between mining and unionism was well established.

The development of the Comstock in the early 1860s marked the beginning of Western underground mining and militant union activity. Apart from the work itself, two features of the Comstock experience shaped hard-rock unionism. Cornish and Irish miners soon dominated the underground labor force, driving out Chinese and Mexican competitors and sparking a wave of violent ethnocentrism. At the same time labor shortages raised wages to $4 per day, establishing a standard that would remain a rallying point for hard-rock miners. The first Comstock union dated from 1862. More durable organizations were formed in 1866 at Gold Hill and in 1867 at Virginia City. Together they were the core of a burgeoning movement based on $4 day and industrial unionism—an approach to organization based on an industry rather than an occupation, geographical area, or other aspect of workplace experience. The Gold Hill constitution became a model for miners' unions throughout the West.

The decline of the Comstock Lode in the late 1870s, together with the success of prospectors in Colorado, Idaho, and adjoining areas, provided an efficient mechanism for the spread of hard-rock organizations. By the mid-1880s there were more than forty local unions with a combined membership of nearly thirty thousand. Few, if any, industries were as completely organized. Emblematic of this development were the formation in 1877 of the Lead City Miners Union and in

1878 of the Butte Miners Union, the "Gibraltar" of hard-rock unionism. Together they assumed the role of the Comstock unions, providing leaders and financial support for fledgling locals.

Yet hard-rock unionism retained its early, parochial character. The miners remained suspicious of eastern European, Mexican, and Chinese workers. They also had little contact with other unions, partly because of the difficulties of travel in the Rocky Mountain West. The Comstock unions formed a regional organization in 1877 to enforce the closed shop, and other nearby locals created similar alliances, but there was no industry-wide organization until the 1890s, when the $4 day came under attack everywhere.

The first major test of the status quo occurred in 1892 at Coeur d'Alene, Idaho Territory. Faced with declining silver prices and intransigent local unions, the operators provoked a strike and imported guards and strikebreakers. The workers were equally determined. In a famous incident they defeated the guards in a struggle that left six dead. Having won the battle, they nearly lost the war. The operators appealed to the territorial governor, who declared martial law and sent federal troops to restore order. Not surprisingly, the soldiers acted as auxiliaries to the operators' forces. They arrested many of the strikers and held them in makeshift "bullpens" for several months, supposedly as a peacekeeping gesture. Still, most miners held out. Finally, after the troops withdrew, the operators and unions agreed to a truce under which the strikers returned to work at their old wages. In the following months both sides prepared for a renewal of the conflict. The collapse of the economy in 1893 gave their preparations a new urgency.

The workers' other response to the Coeur d'Alene conflict was to form a national hard-rock miners union, the Western Federation of Miners (WFM). The Coeur d'Alene operators had demonstrated the effectiveness of an employers' organization; other operators would surely follow their example, attacking isolated local unions. Like many workers of that era, hard-rock miners realized that the whole could be greater than the sum of the parts. From the beginning a handful of large locals, especially the Butte and Lead City organizations, provided a stable membership cadre and a disproportionate share of the WFM's treasury. Their support made it possible for less fortunate miners throughout the American West, Canada, and Alaska to resist the strategy of wage cutting and union avoidance.

Ed Boyce, president from 1896 to 1902, was the principal architect of WFM policy. A veteran of the Coeur d'Alene bullpen, Boyce brought organizational zeal and a radical perspective to his work. Under his stewardship the union took advantage of the economic revival of the late 1890s and soon counted more than twenty thousand members. It also publicly proclaimed its hostility to employers and dedication to class struggle. In 1897 it repudiated the AFL and championed the cause of industrial unionism; eight years later it was instrumental in founding the Industrial Workers of the World, which was to carry its message to workers in other areas and industries. WFM radicalism was a two-edged sword; it helped rally beleaguered miners but also provided operators with a pretext for ruthlessly suppressing union activity.

Although Boyce's revolutionary pronouncements made him famous (and infamous), he was a conservative in one sense. Like other hard-rock union leaders dating from the Comstock era, he paid little attention to the possibilities of collective bargaining. WFM leaders, like their predecessors, were prepared to strike when employers reduced wages or discriminated against union workers. But they retained a parochial, largely negative conception of collective bargaining. The biggest and most successful locals, at Lead City and Butte, did not bargain at all. The day-wage tradition, the industry's partial insulation from market forces, and the isolation of many Western mining communities all contributed to this approach. After all, if everyone worked for the same wage, what was the point of a multiemployer agreement or even a written contract? The point proved to be of the utmost importance. The absence of formal contractual agreements left the locals isolated and defensive, often at the mercy of their employers. The typical WFM local lasted a mere seven years.

Anthracite unionism in the East followed a different course. There was, of course, a heritage of local organization dating from the 1840s. During the Civil War the coal fields became the scene of intense conflict as the military draft and political and ethnic rivalries divided the population into antagonistic factions. Local unions flourished during these years, though none of them was affiliated with the American Miners Association. A series of disastrous 1865 strikes, precipitated by postwar wage reductions, destroyed most of them. The passage of an eight-hour law by the Pennsylvania legislature in 1868 sparked another wave of activism and the emergence of local, county, and regional organizations that by the early 1870s claimed close to fifty thousand members. Unlike the Westerners, anthracite miners were intensely interested in collective bargaining.

The history of the Workingmen's Benevolent Association (WBA)—the loose confederation of anthracite unions—was fraught with conflict. Relations between the locals and their employers were constantly in flux, producing at least one strike every year from 1868 to 1875. Most of these strikes were confined to a particular field, a result of the pattern of mine ownership in the industry. Railroad and canal companies owned most of the mines in the northern field, located in the

Wyoming Valley of northeastern Pennsylvania, while small mining companies dominated the central and southern Lehigh and Schuylkill fields. The transportation companies strongly resisted encroachments on their authority. Although no less suspicious of the workers' organizations, the southern operators were eager to curb competition and raise prices. The Lehigh and Schuylkill unions responded by proposing a sliding scale that tied wages to coal prices. In return they demanded the closed shop and recognition of mine committees. The result was labor management cooperation *and* upheaval, as the mine committees continually struck over nonwage issues.

Complicating the situation was the highly decentralized character of the WBA. A general council, formed in 1869, devoted itself to coordinating the activities of the local and regional organizations. Beneath the general council were county unions, district unions, individual mine organizations, and subdivisions of those organizations. Real power remained in the hands of local leaders and, ultimately, with the rank-and-file miners.

The WBA nevertheless produced one of the legendary figures of the nineteenth-century labor movement, John Siney. Born to impoverished Irish parents, Siney worked in the Lancashire textile industry as a young man and became involved in union activity. Migrating to Pennsylvania in 1863, he settled in the village of St. Clair, in Schuylkill County, and became a miner. When the WBA emerged he was ready for a new career. Siney served successively as president of the St. Clair union, the county union, and the larger WBA; from 1873 to 1876 he was also president of the National Miners Association (NMA), the short-lived second national miners' organization. Siney sought to create a union powerful enough to deal effectively with the operators. He also championed cooperative industry, collective bargaining, and political action, including third-party politics. Distinguished in appearance, moderate in tone, Siney won the confidence of miners and operators. After the collapse of the NMA, he returned to St. Clair and devoted the rest of his life to the Greenback Labor party. At his death in 1880 he was probably the best-known American labor leader.

The collapse of the economy in the mid-1870s exposed the weaknesses of the WBA. Rivalries between northern and southern locals and between Irish, Cornish, and Welsh miners became more pronounced as employers took the offensive. The so-called Long Strike of 1875, involving most WBA organizations, left the union in a shambles. The NMA also collapsed.

Yet this debacle proved to be only a temporary setback. As the economy revived in the late 1870s, unions reemerged and enlisted thousands of miners, though Siney's goal of a powerful unified movement remained elusive. In the anthracite region and in many bituminous fields in Pennsylvania and the Midwest, the Knights of Labor replaced the WBA. In other bituminous fields, state and regional organizations emerged. Relations between the Knights and the independent unions were marred by jealousy and rivalry. In the late 1880s they both sought to create national organizations. Still, many miners and union leaders belonged to both organizations or moved back and forth between them as circumstances changed. On most issues there was no significant difference between them.

Christopher Evans, an English immigrant who began his mining career in the Shenango Valley of western Pennsylvania in 1869, symbolized this continuity. By 1873 Evans was president of the local lodge of the Miners' and Laborers' Benevolent Association, loosely allied with the WBA. During the 1875 strike Evans traveled to the Hocking Valley, in southeastern Ohio, to plead for relief funds. He remained and became a Knights of Labor organizer. He later returned to Pennsylvania but moved back to the Hocking Valley several years later. This time, however, he became active in the independent union that competed with the Knights. Evans's union responsibilities grew rapidly in the following years. In 1889 he was elected secretary-treasurer of the new American Federation of Labor and in 1890 helped form the United Mine Workers of America.

Although the details are obscure, the independent bituminous unions surpassed the Knights during the years when the Knights achieved their greatest following in other industries. The best-documented examples come from Ohio, where a tightly organized industrial union with capable leaders and moderate objectives outmaneuvered the Knights and laid the groundwork for the decisive events of the 1890s.

By the early 1880s the Hocking Valley miners were known for their militancy. They demanded wage adjustments whenever market conditions improved, insisted on union checkweightmen (to assure accurate production records), and opposed company stores. They became the core of the Amalgamated Association of Ohio Miners, founded in 1882. When the operators demanded wage cuts in June 1884, they struck. The bitter conflict continued for eleven months. Despite support from union groups throughout the country, the strikers were soon impoverished. But the operators also suffered. Strikers destroyed several mines and drove out most of the strikebreakers; production was negligible. By the spring of 1885 both sides were exhausted. The miners finally went back to work at the lower rate but refused to disband their organization.

The Hocking miners' struggle had wide repercussions.

Ohio Association president John McBride soon reopened negotiations with the operators. Citing the Hocking debacle as proof of the folly of conflict, McBride persuaded the operators to recognize the union and work with it to resolve disputes. In 1886 he enlisted Ohio Senator Allen Thurman to arbitrate the Hocking wage dispute. This process, much in the tradition of John Siney, was a harbinger of the elaborate bargaining that became the hallmark of union-management relations in the bituminous industry. Meanwhile McBride and the Ohio Association leaders joined Illinois and Indiana leaders and others to form the National Federation of Miners and Mine Laborers, the most important antecedent of the United Mine Workers.

These events put the Knights on the defensive. In response they formed National Trade District No. 135 in May 1886 to coordinate the activities of their many miners' assemblies. William H. Bailey of Ohio became master workman. Leaders of the National Federation and Trade District No. 135 met in Indianapolis in September to consider an alliance, but were unable to resolve their differences. Thereafter their relations deteriorated rapidly. Andrew Roy reported that "the quarrels and bickerings extended to nearly every coal mine in America . . . the opposing miners frequently using their strong right arms to prove the superiority of their respective organizations." The rivalry hurt both unions. Chastened, the leaders resolved again to work together. In 1890 they merged the two organizations, forming the United Mine Workers. National Federation leaders dominated the new union.

McBride became the central figure in the early history of the UMW. Born in rural Ohio, he found work in the nearby Tuscarawas field and at eighteen became a charter member of the local union. He was an officer by the early 1870s and helped negotiate an 1874 arbitration agreement. Blacklisted in

1876, he returned to mining as the economy revived. In 1882 he won the presidency of the Ohio Association and in 1884 and 1886 ran successfully as a Democrat for the state senate. In 1889 he was elected president of the National Federation and in 1892 of the UMW. He brought to the organization highly developed political skills, a commitment to collective bargaining, and an understanding of the economics of the industry.

Within a few months of his election, McBride faced challenges that would have taxed a more experienced leader. The UMW was still in an embryonic state: the anthracite fields remained outside the new organization, and the newer bituminous fields, particularly in southern Appalachia, were largely unorganized. The onset of the 1893 depression created additional problems. The first wage cuts came in the Hocking Valley, the union's heart. By early 1894 they had fueled a rank-and-file rebellion. Militants won important subordinate offices and forced McBride to devise a strike plan. His success in preserving the union during the ensuing conflict was a turning point in the union's history. Three years later his successor called a similar strike, involving more than 160,000 miners. The UMW was stronger this time because of an improving economy, and the operators soon settled. In January 1898 union and employer representatives met in Chicago and negotiated wage scales for mines in an area extending from western Pennsylvania to Kansas, the so-called Central Competitive Field. Probably the most important union achievement of the century, the 1898 accord realized McBride's goal of a stable, peaceful Midwestern industry.

By the end of the nineteenth century American miners had created two formidable national unions and ensured that the workers' voice would be heard in the more prosperous years that followed. Given the workers' devotion to the "principle

of combination," the issue was not whether they could command broad support but whether they could translate that
support into an enduring presence and an impact on the mining industry. In no other industry were union growth and
union structure so interdependent. In the following years the
histories of the UMW and the WFM would diverge radically
as they confronted new and often daunting challenges.

# 3

# Urban Workers and Organized Labor

THE SECOND PATH to union organization ran through the fast-growing cities, where old and new forms of production coexisted uneasily. Artisans in manufacturing and construction formed the earliest city unions to defend traditional prerogatives and living standards. After mid-century they were joined by workers from new occupations in transportation and manufacturing. Regardless of occupation, union members were typically autonomous workers who enjoyed an unusual degree of security because of their skills and their ability to find new jobs with a minimum of delay. Other urban workers remained outside the labor movement. They were a continual source of concern to union leaders and activists. Conservatives emphasized the difficulty of organizing them while critics of inaction evoked the miners' experiences to support demands for a more expansive and aggressive posture.

## PERSPECTIVE: 1888

In February 1888 the engineers and firemen of the Chicago, Burlington & Quincy Railroad and its subsidiaries struck over demands for improvements in the company's wage and promotion plans. One of more than a thousand strikes of the mid-

1880s—a total that marked that decade as the high point of nineteenth-century labor activism—the Burlington strike was arguably the most important railroad strike of that contentious era and one of the most important of the century. Ultimately it cost the strikers their jobs and set back the cause of railroad organization. But the strike has other claims on our attention. It illuminated the position of elite workers in the nineteenth-century labor movement and the conflicts over occupational identity and union jurisdiction that made unified action difficult.

In the 1880s the Brotherhood of Locomotive Engineers (BLE) was a powerful, well-organized union, probably the best example of the ability of elite workers to organize *and* bargain successfully with employers. It was the preeminent example of a national union at a time when most unions were local or regional. Formed in 1863, the BLE had initially emphasized benevolent activities. During the depression of the 1870s it became more aggressive, striking employers who arbitrarily cut wages. Criticism of BLE president Charles Wilson for failing to aid striking engineers led to the election in 1874 of Peter M. Arthur. Under Arthur, who would dominate the BLE for the rest of the century, the union developed a national membership and a commitment to "arbitration," or collective bargaining.

Arthur and his associates had advantages that relatively few organizers enjoyed: their constituents were not only skilled but indispensable. They were at the forefront of the industrial revolution, operating the most vital and demanding machines of the age. No one questioned their claim to high wages; no employer doubted their ability to paralyze a railroad or the disastrous consequences of replacing them with poorly trained substitutes. Arthur himself personified responsibility and business values. A fierce opponent of strikes, he offered employers stability in exchange for high wages and favorable working conditions. Many employers saw the logic of such a bargain. In the late 1870s and 1880s the BLE concluded wage agreements with most major railroads; by the time of the Burlington strike it may have included half of all employed engineers, a remarkable record for the time. It conducted no strikes between 1877 and 1888, an equally exceptional record.

Under Arthur the BLE retained its original, narrow jurisdiction. It was a union of engineers and engineers alone. It excluded even firemen, who worked side by side with engineers, often as apprentice engineers. When firemen formed the Brotherhood of Locomotive Firemen in 1873, BLE leaders were condescending and hostile. They were equally contemptuous of the conductors' and brakemen's organizations and uniformly antagonistic to the Knights of Labor, which organized thousands of railroad employees in the 1880s. These parochial distinctions would play a prominent role in the Burlington strike. They also raised larger issues: should unions be based on single occupations, closely related occupations, or no particular occupation? The miners had chosen a multioccupational jurisdiction, the Knights of Labor a combination of approaches. The BLE confined itself to a single exclusive occupation. Which approach was more promising? The most immediate and relevant answer depended in large measure on the Burlington managers.

Even though the Burlington was one of the largest corporations in the world, it had not yet adopted the internal hallmarks of a big business. It had a comparatively small administrative corps and was run like a collection of small entities. Charles Perkins, the president, delegated most authority to his subordinates, giving them in turn absolute authority over their own subordinates. At their discretion, Burlington managers could enter wage agreements with the BLE and

BLF as long as they did not formally recognize either organization. To Perkins and most of his fellow executives, unions were anathema. A strike was an attack on property as well as an act of insubordination.

The 1888 strike began ostensibly over the company's practice of paying lower wages to new engineers for the first three years and promoting exclusively from within. The beginner's wage encouraged managers to discharge veteran engineers in favor of newcomers, and the promotion policy made it impossible for veterans to regain their jobs after they had been laid off. Exacerbating the conflict were the managers' failures to address workers' grievances promptly and the emergence of a militant faction in the BLE lodges. Unhappy with the company's dilatory tactics, on February 27 the militants struck. To the surprise of Burlington managers and BLE leaders, the strike quickly spread. Within a day or two a thousand engineers and firemen had quit work, bringing Burlington operations to a halt and presenting President Arthur and BLF leaders with a *fait accompli*. They reluctantly supported the walkout. From that point the strike revolved around two issues: the company's effort to recruit strikebreakers, and the strikers' effort to recruit allies among Burlington employees and other railroad workers.

The company had the easier task. Union officials soon learned, to their dismay, that there was no shortage of willing engineers and firemen. The Burlington set up recruiting offices in Chicago and other nearby locations and employed the Pinkerton Detective Agency to recruit Eastern workers. Many men who had lost their jobs were eager to return. Conductors and brakemen also seized the opportunity to move up. Most troubling was the wholesale influx of Knights of Labor members, partly in retaliation for the BLE's failure to support KOL strikes against the Gould Lines in 1886 and the Reading

Railroad in 1887. For several years the Burlington had systematically fired Knights, but in early March it announced that replacement workers, regardless of previous affiliation, would be permanent employees. In mid-March the company changed its seniority rules to favor them over returning strikers.

In addition to replacement workers, the company employed hundreds of Pinkerton detectives and guards. Undercover operatives quickly infiltrated the BLE. They were implicated in a dynamite plot that led to the prosecution of several BLE officials. Another spy became a close friend of President Arthur. Even more provocative were the six hundred uniformed guards hired to protect railroad property. Armed guards were an invitation to violence, as many contemporary miners' strikes typically demonstrated. The Burlington strike was no exception to this pattern. Four strikers died and many were wounded in altercations between guards and strikers during March and April.

As the Burlington hired new workers, the strikers' prospects increasingly depended on their ability to recruit allies. Their goal was to persuade engineers on other railroads to boycott Burlington cars, thus bringing Burlington operations to a halt. Although managers of several rival railroads covertly encouraged their employees to comply, others threatened to fine or discharge cooperating engineers. Meanwhile the company obtained a court injunction banning the boycott and creating a precedent that would become more important in the following years. The BLE was only marginally more successful in enlisting other Burlington employees. The switchmen agreed to strike in return for promises of financial support, but the brakemen refused. Like the engineers and firemen, the switchmen lost their jobs.

By April the strike had been broken. BLE and BLF officials urged the strikers to give up the struggle in order to save their jobs, but in vain. The vast majority of the engineers, firemen, and brakemen never again worked for the Burlington. On the other hand, Perkins and his Burlington associates derived little satisfaction from their victory. Apart from the costs of guards and detectives, revenues declined and the Burlington's competitors benefited. In 1888 the company suffered a substantial loss. The conflict reemphasized a point that Perkins already knew too well: a strike, like a natural disaster, guaranteed losses. Belatedly acknowledging the importance of employee morale, the company soon introduced a relief department, modeled after the insurance plans that Eastern railroads had pioneered. This innovation was one small step toward the systematic management of personnel that corporations like the Burlington embraced after the turn of the century.

The strike's effects on the labor movement are harder to interpret. It provoked a brief revolt against Peter Arthur, his conservative union associates, and the occupational particularism they preached. Arthur's enemies underestimated him, however. By the end of 1888 he had outmaneuvered them, won reelection, and sabotaged their plan for a federation of railroad unions. In the following years he became an even more determined opponent of strikes and mass action. The railroad industry, like most urban industries, would continue to be organized on narrow occupational lines or not at all.

## BEGINNINGS

For two-thirds of a century before the Burlington strike, American workers had organized to advance their interests as wage earners. The overwhelming majority had been male workers who enjoyed a high degree of workplace autonomy,

either classic artisans or skilled machine operators such as locomotive engineers. Their unions grew in prosperous years,
flourished in inflationary periods, and collapsed in recessions.
Regardless of economic conditions, they faced the strenuous
opposition of employers, who, like Perkins, equated organization with disloyalty.

Union activity was closely related to the acceleration of
American economic growth in the early nineteenth century
and the structural changes that accompanied it. At the micro-
economic level, the industrial revolution featured a proliferation of specialized industries and firms. Within the firm
a parallel process created a host of new jobs. In goods-
producing industries, the mechanization of production was
the principal stimulus to job proliferation. A factory or railroad embraced dozens or even hundreds of different jobs. Yet
it is important not to exaggerate the speed of change. These
developments occurred within a single lifetime, but they did
not occur overnight. At any given time, old and new forms of
production operated side by side. The historian Richard Stott
notes that until the 1850s most manufacturing firms in New
York City still did not have subordinate managers. Until the
1880s factories with more than a hundred employees were
oddities. It was the relentless pace of change, more than its
speed, that marked the era. Understandably, contemporary
workers were unsure of their situation and what to do about
it. One choice was to organize and speak with a single voice. A
substantial minority chose this option.

In their pioneering *History of Labour*, John R. Commons
and his students characterized the labor movement as a response to a changing environment. Until the end of the eighteenth century, they argued, "the interests of the small
merchant, employer, and journeyman were identical." Only
after the Constitution of 1787 "and its leveling down of mar-

ket barriers" did a new era of competition arise, separating the
interests of the merchant from those of the manufacturer and
those of the worker. The manufacturer became a contractor
for the merchant. "His main source of profit was his ability to
reduce the prices which he paid for labour." Wage cuts in turn
"drove the wage-earner . . . to his first conscious union with
competing labourers in defense against the master-workman
who had now become the 'boss.' " This interpretive frame-
work, elaborated at length in the first volume of Commons's
work, profoundly influenced subsequent histories. Recent
studies have suggested important modifications.

First and most important, Commons erred in assuming an
identity of interests between pre-Revolutionary artisans and
masters. Class distinctions had appeared in the colonial era
and grew as the economic and social distance between local
elites and other citizens became more obvious. Some masters
undoubtedly identified with their journeymen, but others
were drawn into the merchants' orbit and shared their preten-
sions, a development that Commons associated with a later
period. By disrupting day-to-day activities, creating opportunities for dissidents, and promoting representative government based on a large electorate of equals, the revolutionary
ferment accentuated these distinctions. By the 1790s many
urban artisans subscribed to what historians have termed artisanal republicanism, an adaptation of the national political
ideology. Artisanal republicanism affirmed the worth of the
small producer, the evils of parasitic nonproducers, the dan-
gers of tyrannical power, and the equality of all citizens. For
the next half-century these ideas provided an intellectual
foundation for worker activism in the political arena and in
the workplace. Immigrants subscribed to them no less than
natives.

Two other problems grew out of the limited economic data

available to Commons and his students. First, a dynamic economy enlarged markets, increased competition, and distinguished between producers who embraced entrepreneurial roles and others who became wage earners; but it did not explain the timing or focus of early union activity. If economic growth alone had been the causative agent, the first great upsurge of union activism would have occurred well before the 1830s. Second, Commons underestimated the virulence of the inflationary price spiral of the 1830s, which translated the accumulated tensions of the era into a brief but powerful labor uprising. By reducing the real wages of vulnerable workers, inflation remained one of the most powerful stimuli to union growth.

In short, by the early nineteenth century the urban labor force included a large number of individuals who depended on wages and perceived their welfare as different from and in some respects opposed to that of their employers. Although their activism often took political forms, organization by occupation was an option that became increasingly popular. The choice depended on conditions in particular industries.

Artisans' unions dated from the last decade of the eighteenth century and by the early nineteenth century were common among shoemakers, printers, and other crafts. Their overriding goal was to set wages at levels that enabled members to make a suitable living. Periodically (before the busy season in such trades as construction) union members would draw up a wage list, submit it to their employers, and strike those who refused to pay. To ensure that *most* employers agreed to the list, unions had to limit the availability of nonmembers. Their usual tactics included restrictions on the number of apprentices, restraints on subcontracting, and the closed shop. These exercises of monopoly power were highly controversial, pitting them not only against employers but against nonmembers and less-skilled workers who sought to learn the trade. Employers responded by organizing and instituting suits under the common law against conspiracies, a tactic that proved highly successful. Many unions failed to achieve their goals, and even the most successful lasted only a few years.

Commons dated the urban labor movement from 1827, when Philadelphia artisans formed the Mechanics Union of Trade Associations, a city central or union of unions. The Mechanics Union was better known for its sponsorship of a short-lived Workingman's party than for its union activities. It was involved in neither strikes nor collective bargaining, and in 1831 it disappeared. Nevertheless it served as a model for artisans in other cities. In 1833 New York unions formed a General Trades Union (GTU); shortly thereafter Philadelphia unions organized a new central body; and by the middle of the decade most other cities had comparable organizations. Trades unions continued to dabble in politics, but their principal function was to aid individual unions, especially during strikes. They managed the unions' relations with city officials, organized rallies and other public meetings, and published labor-oriented papers. They were so successful that their leaders formed a National Trades Union—an organization of city organizations—which met from 1834 to 1837. In the longer term they persuaded union leaders of the desirability of local (later county and state) associations which addressed issues of common concern.

Meanwhile, after 1833 and especially after 1835 the number of local unions, members, and strikes grew rapidly. In Philadelphia the number of local organizations increased from twenty-one in 1833 to fifty-three in 1836; in New York it rose from twenty-nine to fifty-two. Since most trades had a single local, this proliferation was a measure of the spread of organization between industries. Workers in the highly competitive consumer goods industries usually took the lead. The appearance of organizations in unrelated trades, many of which, like construction, remained local monopolies, was an indication of the enthusiasm their activities generated. Although inflation was a universal stimulus, the sense of opportunity created by the shoemakers' and tailors' successes reinforced its effects.

The workers' demands also reflected their new confidence. In addition to wage increases, they now demanded a ten-hour day. Reducing the hours of labor would limit competition and create more jobs, they argued, but would also increase the workers' leisure hours and preserve their status as middle-class citizens with time for politics, religion, and other noneconomic pursuits.

By the mid-1830s the journeymen's example began to influence other workers. In Philadelphia the coal heavers initiated the 1835 ten-hour campaign with a spontaneous walkout. Organized construction workers soon joined, and other crafts followed, creating an alliance that cut across skill lines. The Philadelphia trades union admitted representatives of laborers' unions, including the coal heavers. New York unions were more conservative. They acknowledged the importance of the sailors, stevedores, and coal heavers' unions, but did not admit representatives of those groups to the GTU.

The most intriguing possibilities were potential alliances between artisans' unions and factory workers. Between 1828 and 1836 workers in virtually every factory production center struck to protest wage reductions or other indignities. These conflicts arose from the same combination of economic and noneconomic concerns that agitated journeymen. Most of the strikers' organizations were short-lived and quickly forgotten, but there were exceptions. In 1833, Manayunk, Pennsylvania, operatives conducted the longest and best-organized factory strike of that era. Calling themselves the Working People of Manayunk, they issued statements to the press and contacted journeymen's unions in Philadelphia. Immigrant mule spinners who had been involved in earlier English conflicts led the strike. In September 1833, when the strike was a month old, they rallied workers from other nearby factory communities to form the Trades Union of Pennsylvania. Although the strike and the union soon collapsed, the militants were not defeated. They struck again in 1834, winning a wage increase.

Other factory workers followed their example. In 1835 Paterson, New Jersey, textile workers formed the Paterson Association for the Protection of the Labouring Classes and struck for the eleven-hour workday. They counted two thousand supporters from twenty mills. After more than a month of idleness, the strikers agreed to a twelve-hour day, a reduction from the prestrike standard of thirteen and a half hours. A few months later more than two thousand Lowell mill workers formed a Factory Girls Association and struck against increased boardinghouse charges. Their strike lasted more than two months.

By 1836 the total number of artisans, laborers, and factory operatives who had organized was substantial. A contemporary publication estimated that in 1834 there were 26,000 union members. Commons cites another estimate in 1836 of 300,000 members. Judging from the number of unions, it is more likely that membership peaked at two to three times the 1834 total, or between 50,000 and 70,000, an impressive figure given the meager experience of most workers, the absence of regional or national unions, and the indifference or hostility of most local governments.

In any case, the unions of the 1830s depended greatly on the inflationary economy. With the financial panic of 1837, prices collapsed, businesses closed, and workers lost their jobs or suffered substantial wage cuts. Almost without exception their unions also disappeared. Since most labor newspapers collapsed at the same time, it is probably impossible to know how many union members there were after the mid-1830s. Whatever the total, their influence was negligible.

The antebellum labor movement would never again regain the membership, visibility, or élan it had in the mid-1830s. Organizations of artisans and factory workers reappeared and strikes were common, but most activity was local and sporadic. To contemporaries it seemed devoid of larger significance. Stable prices, a rapidly expanding economy, and mounting immigration all contributed to this situation.

## EXPANSION AND CHANGE, 1860S–1870S

Unlike the preceding quarter-century, the years from the early 1860s to the mid-1890s were years of dramatic union expansion and redefinition, as workers adapted to the opportunities and perils of a rapidly growing and industrializing economy. The story of the mining industries provides the most compelling evidence of this process, but urban workers played major roles as well. After the 1830s the factory became increasingly an urban institution, adding a new element to the urban labor force and a new type of industrial district. By mid-century railroads dominated intercity transportation, employing more workers than any other firms. To fill the new jobs, a growing stream of immigrants, mostly Anglo-Irish or German, settled in Northern cities. Their presence was evidence of the growing efficiency of the labor market. Yet greater mobility also meant that workers had greater difficulty creating and sustaining local labor monopolies, especially when employers sought to increase the supply of

potential employees. Gradually union leaders began to realize
that only regional or even national organizations would enable them to achieve their goals.

The shoeworkers of eastern Massachusetts inaugurated the
new era with the largest American strike to date. Twenty
thousand wage earners, half the industry total, struck for six
weeks in February and March 1860. Low wages were the immediate cause. As the Lynn strikers proclaimed, the manufacturers were "grinding us down so low that men with large
families could not live within their means." Beneath the sur-
face, however, were anxieties about the likely fate of hand-
workers in a world of machines and factories. After several
clashes between strikers and nonstrikers, which led the governor to call out the militia, the strike became an endurance contest. The strikers were ill-equipped for a prolonged siege.
Hunger and the prospect of losing their jobs to strikebreakers
drove the workers back in April. Yet this apparent defeat
proved only a temporary setback. In the following years, as
factories replaced hand operations, former artisans realized
that mechanization and specialization did not obliterate skill
distinctions or substantially lessen their shop-floor autonomy.
And by physically concentrating employees and standardizing
wages and working conditions, factories could actually contribute to organization. From the 1860s to the turn of the century, shoemaking would be the most highly organized
manufacturing industry.

Meanwhile the shoeworkers—and other industrial workers—had to deal with the effects of the Civil War. By encouraging or forcing thousands of young workers to enter the
army and discouraging immigration, the war created labor
shortages and pressures for higher wages. At the same time
the Lincoln administration raised taxes and issued fiat money
(the famous greenbacks) to finance the war. The result was a

rapid rise in prices and a fall in real wages. Economists are uncertain whether industrial workers were the principal victims of this squeeze, but they agree that higher prices erased the positive effects of the labor shortage. Nor were there offsetting benefits. Unlike later wartime governments, the Lincoln administration made no effort to encourage production or avoid strikes. Indeed, its ill-managed conscription policies and readiness to use armed force to break strikes reflected a remarkable insensitivity to the problems of the industrial labor force.

Organization was thus a defensive response to a hostile environment. Because of the labor shortage, it was also a low-risk response: organizers or activists who lost their jobs found new positions with little trouble. Coal miners and elite urban workers led the way. A contemporary report estimated that by 1865 there were 1,500 local, regional, and national unions. By the early 1870s the labor movement had at least 300,000 members, the largest total to date. Miners accounted for nearly one-third of the total, followed by shoemakers, iron workers, and urban artisans—printers, tailors, construction workers, and others. In the largest cities longshoremen, hod carriers, teamsters, and other laborers also organized.

By 1864 unions in large and mid-sized cities were numerous enough to form city federations. The New York City Workingmen's Assembly, with hundreds of constituent unions and tens of thousands of members, was the most formidable American labor organization. Assemblies provided financial and political support for strikes, published newspapers, and spearheaded political campaigns for the eight-hour day and bans on prison-made goods. In 1866 they formed the National Labor Union (NLU), which met annually until 1875 (from 1873 to 1875 as the Industrial Congress). The NLU provided a national forum for union leaders and a mechanism for coordinating political and legislative campaigns. It also signaled a growing realization that some issues transcended occupations and geography.

If the unionists of the post–Civil War years failed to influence national politics, they were more successful in other venues. The quintessential labor institution of that era was the local union, consisting of workers in a single occupation in a single locality, affiliated (at least in larger cities) with a trades assembly. The local could be highly effective, but its isolation from the rest of the industry in which its members worked, heretofore largely irrelevant, could now be a serious shortcoming. The problem was most obvious and probably most severe in transportation and manufacturing, where firm size and employer power were growing and where competition was increasingly regional or even national, meaning that wages and other labor standards were constantly subject to outside influences. But even in local market industries such as construction, isolation was not complete. The rapid extension of the railroad network made every town accessible to unemployed workers, immigrants, and strikebreakers. The isolated local was increasingly vulnerable.

The answer was obvious: a larger entity with the organizational resources to confront the effects of a growing and modernizing economy. In the 1830s printers, shoemakers, and other artisan unions had attempted to create national organizations, but none of them survived the subsequent recession. Renewed efforts in the 1850s floundered during the recession of 1857. On the eve of the Civil War the roster of national unions included the stonecutters, hat finishers, molders, and machinists. Yet they were, in the words of the historian Norman Ware, "national in name only." A decade later there were more than thirty national unions, ranging from the powerful American Miners Association and the Knights of St. Crispin

to the small, obscure Horseshoers. Many were weak and inef-
fective, ill-equipped to withstand the depression of the mid-
1870s. Yet the model had been firmly established. Henceforth
the national union, representing workers throughout the
United States (and often Canada), would remain the basic unit
of the American labor movement.

Within this context the rise of national unions did not follow a predictable pattern. We have already traced the early
history of the Locomotive Engineers. The experience of the
International Molders Union, the most durable of the factory
workers' organizations, provides additional perspective.
Molders locals, representing mostly stove foundry workers,
dated from the 1820s and 1830s but did not become an important force in the industry until the mid-1850s. Workers in the
major foundry centers organized to raise wages or to prevent
reductions. By 1857 they had created sixteen locals, including
large and formidable unions in Philadelphia and Troy, New
York. After three failed strikes in 1859, the Philadelphia local
took the lead in creating a national union. By 1861 the International Molders Union had attracted most of the existing locals, forty-four in all. Two years later the annual meeting
elected William Sylvis, of the Philadelphia local, as president.
Sylvis immediately embarked on an organizing tour that took
him to every foundry center and resulted in the formation of
eighteen additional locals. For the next four years the indefati-
gable Sylvis kept up this pace. Membership peaked in 1867 at
8,600. Sylvis was also a key figure in the formation of the National Labor Union and served as president from 1866 until
his death in 1868. At that time he was the best-known American labor leader.

Like other national unions, the Molders confronted a host
of managerial issues. Should they charge high dues and offer a
variety of benefits and services? Should they have a strong or a

weak national executive? Which powers and functions should remain with the locals? They chose high dues and benefits. The Molders' strike-benefit plan remained a contentious issue for a quarter-century. Only in the 1890s did the national officers finally win control of it. Other issues were resolved in similar fashion. The exigencies of survival in a competitive environment dictated this cautious, evolutionary approach.

In contrast to the BLE and the Molders, the Knights of St. Crispin achieved record membership among shoeworkers without prolonged soul-searching or internal turmoil. The KSP had deep roots in Massachusetts and New Hampshire shoemaking communities and in the prewar labor movement. Nevertheless by the late 1860s it was a union of factory workers with no restrictions on eligibility. Although the elite cutters remained aloof and the women employees formed parallel organizations called the Daughters of St. Crispin, the Crispin locals were de facto industrial unions. At their peak, around 1870, they embraced as many as fifty thousand workers. Like the typical shoe factory, the Knights of St. Crispin was decentralized and depended largely on local initiative.

Crispin leaders emphasized formal agreements with employers. Whereas most unions—regardless of national affiliation—continued to present their demands to employers and strike if they were refused, the Crispins opted for formal wage bargains, negotiated with representatives of employers' groups. A favorable 1870 contract underlined the advantages of this approach. Later contracts were less successful, and a disastrous 1878 strike left the union in disarray. Yet the collapse of the Crispins was no more inhibiting than the loss of the 1860 shoeworkers' strike. Within a year or two most Crispin lodges had reorganized as assemblies of the Knights of Labor. Like the coal miners, they were less interested in the union's name than in its ability to represent their interests.

Most unions of the 1870s were less fortunate. During the depression of 1873–1877 unemployment rose, wages fell, and many organizations declined. Either they lost most of their members to layoffs or, like the anthracite miners, struck unsuccessfully to maintain existing wage levels. Half the national unions disappeared, and total membership fell by three-quarters or more. The Typographical Union, one of the few national unions to survive the recession of 1857, declined from 106 locals and 9,800 members in 1874 to 69 locals and 4,300 members in 1878. The Molders declined from 127 locals and 7,500 members in 1874 to 83 locals and 2,900 members in 1879. Many others disappeared. Much of the turmoil of the 1870s, notably the famous strikes and riots of 1877, resulted from spontaneous protests, not union agitation.

## THE GREAT UPHEAVAL AND AFTER, 1880s–1897

The disastrous years of the mid-1870s were followed by a boom in union membership that carried the labor movement to unprecedented heights. So great was the increase that veterans of the struggles of the 1860s were amazed that so much was possible so quickly and, relatively speaking, so effortlessly. Historians, no less impressed, have typically portrayed the 1880s as unique, especially because of the prominence of the Knights of Labor, which surpassed all other national unions in membership—only to collapse and virtually disappear by the early 1890s. Conflicts between national unions and the Knights, and between Terence V. Powderly, grand master workman of the Knights, and Samuel Gompers, president of the new American Federation of Labor, accentuated the apparent distinctiveness of the union experience in the 1880s. In retrospect, however, it is the continuity between the experiences of the postwar years and the 1880s and early 1890s that stands out. The major themes of the "great upheaval" included the growing dominance of national unions, the emergence of union executives who rivaled leading employers in visibility and influence, the maturing of the union as a political organization, the spread of collective bargaining, and a growing sophistication in union pressure techniques, all of which had important antecedents in earlier years. The fate of the BLE in 1888 was a reminder that progress was not automatic. Still, the survival and continued expansion of the BLE after the Burlington strike was an indication of how much had been accomplished since the 1860s.

The Knights of Labor, which dated from 1869, was the great success story of the 1870s and early 1880s. By late 1873 the KOL had more than eighty locals, comparable to many national unions. Unlike other unions, however, it organized workers from all industries and included "mixed" locals of workers from different industries. The first ten KOL locals, all in Philadelphia, were composed of garment cutters, ship carpenters, shawl weavers, carpet weavers, ship riggers, stove masons, bag makers, machinists, and stonecutters. In 1874 the KOL spread to New York, New Jersey, and Massachusetts and began to create "district assemblies" of locals, much like the trades assemblies. Although many local assemblies collapsed in the following years, the KOL did not disappear. Its resiliency reflected an inclusive, pragmatic approach to organization. In particular, it successfully recruited thousands of coal miners after the collapse of the Workingmen's Benevolent Association and many shoeworkers after the decline of the Knights of St. Crispin. By 1878, when the KOL held its first general assembly, or national convention, it was poised for renewed growth.

During the generally prosperous decade and a half that followed, many groups began a "search for order" that empha-

sized restraints on market forces and an expanded public sector. Railroads merged; manufacturers created cartels; farmers
formed a variety of "alliances"; and professionals formed their
own associations. Industrial workers also sought protection
from labor market competition through an institutional voice.
Unions grew by merging, by absorbing isolated locals, and by
recruiting unorganized workers, including former members.
Dramatic membership gains were common. Between 1879
and 1886 the Molders experienced a sixfold increase; between
1879 and 1884 the KOL grew eightfold.

Like other occupational groups, unions confronted mounting internal problems as they grew. The most obvious and
pressing of these was the character of their professional staffs.
Should national officers be part-time or full-time? How much
should they be paid? William Sylvis had nearly starved in the
1860s, and Peter McGuire, the idealistic president of the Carpenters, subsisted on a meager salary. By the 1890s, however,
national union officers demanded better treatment. In most
cases the secretary or secretary-treasurer, burdened with a
growing volume of record-keeping and correspondence, was
the first full-time employee. Other officers followed. Most of
them, like Peter Arthur, Powderly, and Gompers, were indistinguishable from merchants, bankers, and other upstanding
citizens.

Other issues were more perplexing. Locomotive engineers,
lasters, and loom fixers were readily indentifiable, but what
precisely was a carpenter or an iron worker? In the 1830s
trade boundaries had not been a serious problem. But by the
1880s many traditional trades had declined and a host of new
occupations had appeared. Although miners solved this problem by organizing everyone who worked in the industry, most
urban workers continued to organize by occupation. This approach raised other questions. Some jobs were occupationally

ambiguous, incorporating features of several trades; others had only some features of a particular occupation. Given the occupational particularism of most unions, disputes over jurisdiction were inevitable; in the railroad and construction industries, where narrowly defined organizations were the rule, they became endemic.

The skill issue presumably was less formidable: most unions continued to exclude laborers, though on occasion they helped low-skill workers form separate organizations. Still, there were problems, especially in factories where workers performed repetitive and relatively easy-to-master machine operations. Unions of factory workers, such as the Crispins, the Amalgamated Association of Iron and Steel Workers, and the Brotherhood of Operative Potters, continually revised their definition of skilled work to include the less-skilled, particularly those who played strategic roles in the production process.

### KNIGHTS OF LABOR LOCAL ASSEMBLIES, DISTRIBUTION BY INDUSTRY

(percent of total)

| Industry | Pa. | Mass. | Ill. |
|---|---|---|---|
| Service | 3 | 8 | 10 |
| Construction | 3 | 6 | 4 |
| Transportation | 2 | 4 | 2 |
| Mining | 43 | <1 | 23 |
| Mixed | 19 | 23 | 35 |
| Manufacturing | 30 | 58 | 25 |
| Clothing | 2 | 2 | 4 |
| Tobacco | 2 | 2 | 1 |
| Boots, Shoes | 2 | 24 | <1 |
| Iron, Steel | 5 | <1 | 2 |
| Textiles | 4 | 7 | <1 |
| Number | 1297 | 434 | 568 |

The KOL addressed those issues by organizing all workers in a single overarching national body with a variety of local forms. The preceding table lists local assemblies by occupation in three major industrial states and illustrates the effects of this policy. In Pennsylvania the KOL was primarily an organization of miners; in Massachusetts of shoeworkers; and in Illinois of factory workers. Yet there were many other assemblies in every state as well as "mixed" or multioccupational assemblies.

Kim Voss's study of the KOL in New Jersey provides the most precise accounting of the Knights' growth.

GROWTH OF THE KNIGHTS OF LABOR IN NEW JERSEY

(C=Craft; LS=Less-Skilled; Ind=Industrial; Mixed)

|  | C | LS | Ind | Mixed |
|---|---|---|---|---|
| 1873–1878 | 7 | 0 | 2 | 1 |
| 1879–1885 | 30 | 34 | 12 | 16 |
| 1886 | 36 | 60 | 72 | 24 |
| 1887–1895 | 10 | 12 | 7 | 0 |

Until the late 1870s the New Jersey Order consisted largely of skilled workers. As the pace of organization increased in the 1880s, it expanded to include assemblies of factory workers (the less-skilled), a few industrial unions (mostly in manufacturing; mining was unimportant in New Jersey), and a large number of mixed locals (which were often small-town locals of elite workers from different trades). In 1886, with the KOL and the labor movement at high tide, most organizations were multioccupational. After 1886, as the Knights faced more intense opposition and it became apparent that membership was not riskless, relatively few new industrial or mixed locals appeared. Except for the 1886 boom, the industrial and mixed locals would have been a small, unimportant fragment of the New Jersey KOL.

The most intriguing feature of the New Jersey data is the prominence of factory workers. They were present in each category, though the majority were in the less-skilled group. Voss reports that 61 percent of New Jersey KOL members were in manufacturing and that the total in machinery and metals, and in textiles, both exceeded every nonmanufacturing industry. Clearly it was not just molders, machinists, potters, and glassblowers who sought a collective voice. But given their limited skills and autonomy, how were factory workers to organize?

Elite organizations played a major role. As skilled-worker unions grew, they often encouraged workers in other industries to organize. Regardless of what they thought of less-skilled employees in their own plants and industries, elite workers recognized the advantages of a larger, healthier labor movement. This "community" perspective apparently transcended ethnic distinctions and other factors that often undermined worker unity.

A similar process occurred in other areas. In Detroit, for example, the KOL and other national unions both won victories in the early 1880s. Although aggregate membership grew slowly (from four thousand in 1881 to five thousand in 1885), unions enlisted many nonmembers in successful boycotts against recalcitrant employers. Until 1886 most of these sympathizers held back from joining because of the likelihood of reprisals. Finally, convinced that the balance of power between employers and unions had shifted, thousands of cautious employees cast their lot with the labor movement. Organizers, as the historian Richard Oestreicher reports, realized that "apparently apathetic workers had been listening all along." In Detroit, as in New Jersey, the spring of 1886 was the high-water mark of union organizing in the nineteenth century.

In many areas, however, there were no unions to serve as catalysts. In the Southern textile industry and the Michigan lumber industry, where the KOL achieved major breakthroughs, there had been no local organizations before the mid-1880s. Workers reacted to the Knights' reputation for winning strikes. That reputation dated from the winter of 1883–1884, when the KOL window-glass workers won a prolonged strike while other unions (notably the Hocking Valley miners) were losing strikes. In 1884 KOL assemblies of shopcraft workers (machinists, boilermakers, and other workers who repaired locomotives) won two strikes against the Union Pacific Railroad. In 1885 they won two more strikes against the Gould lines; in the second strike KOL negotiators worked out the final settlement directly with Jay Gould, the personification of everything (financial manipulation, speculative profits, contempt for community well-being) the Knights and other unionists professed to hate. Union victory over Gould was symbolically important, especially for factory workers like the shopmen. If the KOL could defeat an employer as powerful, ruthless, and irresponsible as Gould, presumably it could defeat any employer. Fear of reprisals waned and the union impulse broadened to include less-skilled industrial workers across the country.

Many new union members hoped to take advantage of their collective voice by striking. More than twice as many strikes occurred in 1886 as a year earlier; nearly five times as many establishments and two and a half times as many workers were affected. At first the strikes were an expression of the workers' confidence and expectations. But when employers rallied and defeated many of them, they began to represent something quite different: the unions' lack of preparation, faulty leadership, and inadequate resources. Historians have emphasized Powderly's mismanagement of KOL strikes. But Powderly's role is hard to distinguish from that of Peter Arthur or other union executives. What was different was the Knights' lax control of the strike power and meager provisions for strike relief. In 1886 the sheer number of strikes would have strained any system; in the case of the Knights, it undermined the entire organization.

Strike defeats, public hostility, worker disillusionment, and employer reprisals precipitated an exodus from the KOL and from other unions that was almost as dramatic as the 1885–1886 influx. Having risen to 730,000 in 1886, KOL membership fell by nearly two-thirds in the next two years. By 1890 it was only 100,000.

Under attack, KOL members and supporters responded more effectively outside the workplace. Since the era of the National Labor Union, unions had taken an active role in local and state politics, often as promoters of third parties. While their chances of displacing or capturing one of the major parties was no better in the 1880s than in the 1860s, the Greenback campaign of the 1870s demonstrated that third parties could attract voters in local contests. In the early eighties KOL representatives had been active lobbyists. The influx of new members encouraged them to move into the electoral arena. In 1886 and 1887 dozens of local labor parties ran candidates. In large cities coalitions of unions created new parties; in small cities the KOL usually played the leading role. Labor candidates won mayoral contests in Milwaukee and many small communities. Others were elected to city councils and other governing bodies in Chicago, Cincinnati, and other cities.

Yet the labor parties proved to be as ephemeral as the mem-

bership gains. Republicans and Democrats dedicated themselves to defeating the upstarts, and labor officeholders, most
of whom were inexperienced newcomers, failed to fulfill their
supporters' expectations. Most union-backed officials lost
their positions after a single term. By 1890 the major parties
and their veteran unions' were back in control. The most important effect of the leaders' political campaigns was less tan-
gible: they demonstrated the potential of parties based on
union and working-class voters.

To what degree did union disunity contribute to the union
failures? That question has been prominent in analyses of the
events of the 1880s and the decline of the KOL. Until the early
1880s there was no clear line between the KOL and other
unions; members easily moved between organizations, and
many activists held multiple memberships. Unions also affiliated with the KOL or disaffiliated as circumstances changed.
Opportunism and expediency—and a sense of exhilaration
based on their unaccustomed successes—characterized their
behavior. Certainly there were differences between the KOL
and the independent national unions, notably the group that
in late 1886 formed the American Federation of Labor. The
contrast between the views of Powderly and Samuel Gompers
is especially striking. But the similarities among the unions are
also impressive. One of the earliest historians of the KOL,
Norman Ware, wrote, "There was no form of organization
that [the KOL] did not possess at one time or another, no
function it did not perform or attempt, and almost no theory
[it] did not hold either officially or unofficially." That statement applies with equal validity to the AFL unions.

The conflicts that led to the formation of the AFL arose out
of competition for members, not skill distinctions or philo-
sophical differences. While these struggles threatened the in-

dividual organizations, they were not necessarily harmful to the labor movement as a whole. In many cases competition stimulated both sides to organize more aggressively.

The formation of the AFL was an effort by the independent national unions to improve their competitive appeal. KOL organizers could argue that their union was not only national but diverse, able to draw on the resources of many industries. During the spring and summer of 1886, national union leaders tried to devise a cooperative relationship with the KOL that would enable them to make similar claims. Powderly and the KOL leaders, some of whom were personally obnoxious to the other union executives, stalled, giving the impression they would continue to raid other organizations. The impasse played into the hands of anti-KOL militants such as Gompers. At a meeting in Columbus, Ohio, in December 1886, the Gompers group formed the American Federation of Labor. But their achievement should not be exaggerated. For at least a decade the AFL was mostly a public relations gesture: it enabled national union leaders to argue that they were part of a coherent, diverse, and comprehensive movement.

Amid these dramatic events and conflicts it is easy to overlook the fact that during the 1880s national unions registered important gains. One reason was the desertion of KOL unions, such as the coal miners, for the AFL, and the merger of other KOL units, such as the Carpenters' district assemblies, into AFL organizations. The most important gains, however, came from other sources. Construction workers, not factory workers or even miners, responded most effectively to the 1880s environment. They were beneficiaries of the decade's prosperity and labor shortages. Unlike railroad employees, they did not have to worry about the power of big business. Unlike factory workers, they did not have to worry about mechanization or intrusive supervisors. "Tramp" workers, cost-conscious employers, and factories that prefabricated building components were important but not insurmountable challenges. Careful management and mastery of local labor markets were the keys to success.

The Carpenters, soon to be the largest and most formidable urban union, dated from an 1881 consolidation of local unions and grew rapidly in the following years. Peter McGuire, the union's secretary and dominant figure, was the architect of this growth. Under his stewardship the Carpenters won the eight-hour day and were poised to absorb other woodworkers' organizations. Yet for all his achievements, McGuire was increasingly out of step with his constituents. An agitator and socialist, he had little in common with the growing cadre of business agents who looked and acted like the upwardly mobile entrepreneurs they were. In the 1890s McGuire's fortunes declined, and in 1900 he was expelled for stealing union funds. The business agents' triumph was freighted with symbolism. But it also had a more prosaic meaning. Given the intensity of employer opposition, successful union leaders had to understand their industries, recognize opportunities when they arose, and exploit their advantages. Men like Powderly and McGuire, who seemed like throwbacks to an earlier, simpler age, did not inspire confidence.

The Burlington strike, which came at the end of the KOL-inspired strike wave, reinforced this point. The outcome of the strike was depressingly similar to the results of other strikes during that tumultuous era. Yet, unlike the majority of KOL unions, or Eugene Debs's American Railway Union, which collapsed after a famous strike against the Pullman Company in 1894, the Brotherhood of Locomotive Engineers did not disappear after its defeat. It paid strike benefits to all the displaced engineers and retained their allegiance. In the following years it continued to expand, ever more cautious about the use of the strike power. Like the leaders of the building trades unions, the officers of the BLE and the other brotherhoods dressed and acted like the employers they confronted over the negotiating table. Critics accused them of selling out; they replied that they were simply realists. The nature and consequences of their realism would become more apparent in the following years, as both groups of unionists, rural and urban, struggled to master their environment and create a powerful and permanent labor movement.

# 4

# New Environments, New Challenges, 1897–1930

THE POSSIBILITIES of the American labor movement became fully apparent for the first time during the first quarter of the twentieth century. Beginning in 1897, a reinvigorated economy inspired a union revival that recalled many features of the 1880s boom. This revival in turn stimulated a vigorous counteroffensive by employers that eliminated the most vulnerable new unions. By the mid-1910s the labor movement again consisted largely of miners and autonomous industrial workers. World War I shattered the new equilibrium, created unprecedented labor shortages, and led to a dramatic expansion of the public sector. As a result, workers in transportation and manufacturing could largely disregard the threat of reprisals for half a decade. They responded by creating a labor movement larger and more representative than ever before. The end of war mobilization and the return to economic "normalcy" between 1919 and 1922 had predictable effects. Workers became vulnerable to employer reprisals; many local unions collapsed and others, including the old core groups, declined. The failure of the railroad shopcraft unions in a famous 1922 strike was emblematic of this process. By the late 1920s union density had declined to prewar levels, though a collapse like those of the 1870s or 1890s was no more likely than another mobilization of the economy.

### PERSPECTIVE: 1922

On August 18, 1922, President Warren G. Harding addressed a joint session of Congress on the coal and railroad strikes that had idled a million workers for more than a month. Harding's comments on the strike of shopcraft workers were particularly important, for, unlike the miners, the railroad strikers had evoked broad public support. Harding criticized the railroad managers for intransigence, renewed his call for a negotiated settlement, and then attacked the strikers and their organizations. Unions had condoned violence, he charged, including attacks on federal officials; had become as unyielding as their employers; and bore most of the responsibility for the continuation of the nationwide strike. As president he would use his power to "maintain transportation and sustain the right of men to work." Harding's speech signaled the victory of anti-union advisers within his administration. Shortly thereafter he authorized Attorney General Harry Daugherty to obtain a sweeping injunction against the strikers. With the strike already near collapse, the injunction only accelerated the unions' defeat. But Harding's action had a larger meaning: it symbolized the end to a quarter-century of erratic government encouragement for unions and collective bargaining.

The shopcraft strike was an indirect result of the government takeover of the railroads during World War I. Nationalization created a favorable environment for union growth and collective bargaining. Conventional notions of efficiency, based on costs, gave way to a larger sense of national efficiency aimed at successful prosecution of the war. In this setting union leaders had much to offer. In exchange for the freedom to recruit members and bargain without fear of reprisals, they promised uninterrupted service, cooperation, and support for the war effort. It was a favorable arrangement for both sides, marred only by the strident complaints of shippers. Railroad union membership grew from less than 500,000 in 1917 to more than 1 million in 1920. The BLE, BLF, Trainmen, and Conductors each grew by 25 percent or more, but the railroad clerks, maintenance-of-way workers, telegraphers, and other unions of less-skilled and less vital employees all grew by 200 to 500 percent. The Railway Employees Department (RED) of the AFL, which represented the six shopcraft unions, enjoyed a nearly tenfold increase in membership.

The wartime organization of the shopcraft workers, who built and repaired rolling stock, was a telling commentary on railroad industrial relations and the power of large corporations. Railroad shopworkers were skilled, autonomous employees. Each of their jobs was different; many required technical creativity; and intrusive supervision was difficult. In short, shopcraft employees were the kind of industrial worker most likely to organize. They had often tried, but usually with discouraging results. One of the bitterest strikes of the prewar years had involved the shopcrafts of the Harriman lines. In some communities the strike lasted for three years. Managers used the same combination of replacement workers and legal tactics that they had employed against the BLE in 1888, and in the end the strikers conceded defeat. The parochialism of the operating brotherhoods was an impediment, but the employers' power was decisive—until the war created a new and more accommodating environment. With the government in charge, shopcraft workers became eager union recruits.

The Transportation Act of 1920 brought this interlude to an end. The act returned the railroads to their owners, revived

the Interstate Commerce Commission, and created a Railroad
Labor Board to mediate disputes between the largely anti-
union companies and the unions, including the RED. The
board had no enforcement powers. From the beginning it was
unable to persuade railroad managers to abide by decisions
they opposed. Given this hostility and the suspicions of the
unions, the board became wedded to the status quo. On wage
questions it sought to adjust wage rates to living costs. In July
1920, for example, it ordered increases of 22 percent to com-
pensate workers for higher food and housing costs. When the
postwar recession slashed consumer prices, it approved wage
cuts. A reduction of 12.5 percent in May 1921 led to a prolonged confrontation with the unions. Thereafter the board
was more circumspect. It avoided antagonizing the operating
brotherhoods but continued to approve reductions for less
powerful groups. A new round of cuts in June 1922 precipitated the conflict with the shopcrafts.

For most railroad managers the strike was a long-awaited
opportunity to eliminate unions of nonoperating employees.
They hired strikebreakers and guards and in many states se-
cured injunctions to limit picketing. Confrontations between
guards and pickets resulted in a half-dozen striker fatalities.
Governors called out the National Guard in a dozen states. In
late July the companies announced they would abolish seniority rights, which freed them from taking back the strikers.

Although the strike was popular in many railroad centers,
the strikers faced growing, ultimately insurmountable problems. The refusal of the operating brotherhoods and other
unions (including the maintenance-of-way, clerks', and signalmen's organizations) to join the strike made a total cessation of rail service impossible. Although the employers'
intransigence was no surprise, the availability of large numbers of workers with at least some training in engine and

boiler work was. By late July RED leaders concluded that further resistance was fruitless; they offered to accept the wage reduction and return to work. The employers' refusal to negotiate with the unions shifted the spotlight from labor and management to the federal government. What would the Harding administration do to restore service?

The administration's position was complicated by the persistence of the nationwide coal strike, which had started in April. The coal strike resulted from the operators' demands for wage reductions commensurate with the price reductions that had occurred during the recession. They pointed to the growth of low-wage, nonunion fields in West Virginia and the South as a measure of the unrealistic level of wages in the Central Competitive Field and in eastern Pennsylvania. But their fundamental objection was broader: they insisted that the CCF had become obsolete and that only field-by-field agreements, reflecting local competitive conditions, could stabilize employment and profits. To UMW president John L. Lewis and his associates, these demands attacked the very foundation of the union. They rejected any concessions.

By July, Harding and his aides were exasperated with Lewis and concerned about the combined effects of the coal and railroad strikes. On July 18 the president urged governors of coal-producing states to protect strikebreakers and pledged government assistance. Harding's threats had little effect on the course of the coal dispute, which was settled in mid-August with an agreement reaffirming the status quo, but they augured ill for the shopcraft strike. Since the railroad companies held the upper hand in their strike and were adamant about not making concessions, the quickest way to break the impasse was to embrace the employers' solution. Pressures for a resumption of service ultimately dictated the destruction of the shopcraft unions.

Until early August 1922, Secretary of Commerce Herbert Hoover and Secretary of Labor James Davis guided administration policy. Hoover had little regard for the Labor Board and was appalled at the railroad managers' intransigence. When union leaders agreed to call off the strike, he carried their offer to the executives in New York. Their rebuff was a rebuff to him as well. Hoover complained that their "social instinct belonged to an early Egyptian period." From that point his influence waned. The collapse of negotiations encouraged the administration's anti-union conservatives, led by Attorney General Daugherty. At their urging Harding called for the Labor Board to resolve the seniority issue along with other questions. This proposal was wholly unacceptable to the unions. Harding's attacks on the strikers and Daugherty's comprehensive injunction followed.

The strike quickly collapsed. Moderates, led by Daniel Willard of the Baltimore & Ohio, agreed to rehire strikers, seniority intact, at the lower rates proposed by the Labor Board. Approximately 225,000 strikers returned under these terms. Willard also introduced a novel cooperative plan that involved union leaders and workers in shop-floor decision-making. Other strikers were less fortunate. Conservative managers, led by the Pennsylvania Railroad, rehired shopmen as individuals and proclaimed the open shop. Their idea of labor-management cooperation was a company union and an enhanced pension plan.

The shopcraft strike was thus a gauge of the industrial relations climate of the 1920s and of the changes that had occurred since the 1890s. Unions had grown larger and more powerful; they were better led and able to command political support in many states and in Washington. They faced difficult adjustments after World War I, but only because they had achieved so much influence in the preceding quarter-century. Even in the darkest days of 1922, they were incomparably stronger than their nineteenth-century predecessors. Perhaps the best indicator of this change was the persistence of unions in manufacturing, where worker autonomy was often limited and reprisals for union activity were customarily swift and certain. The fact that the shopcraft organizations survived made them symbols of an age.

## MINERS AND INDUSTRIAL RELATIONS, 1897–1915

The issues that troubled Harding, Hoover, shopcraft leaders, and railroad managers originated in the economic revival of the late 1890s. After 1897 production and employment had grown rapidly in all sectors; with only brief interruptions, the years to 1920 would be a period of opportunity and rising incomes for American workers. Even the arrival of more than a million immigrants a year until 1914 did not significantly reduce employment opportunities or halt the growth of real wages. As in other periods of rising incomes and rising prices, good times encouraged industrial workers to seek a formal voice. With few exceptions they turned to national unions. Employers responded with open-shop organizations. Both sides then turned to government for assistance. The unpredictable effects of this process were nowhere more apparent than in the mining industries, the traditional heart of the labor movement.

By the late 1890s the United Mine Workers and the Western Federation of Miners were poised for renewed growth. Encouraged by the great strikes of 1894 and 1897, UMW activists took advantage of the new prosperity to create the largest American union and the most important AFL affiliate. Their experiences underlined the possibilities of the era. Yet the margin between growth and decline, success and failure,

remained narrow. The surprising fate of the WFM attested to
the precarious condition of even the strongest union. In the
mid-1890s the WFM probably had a larger membership than
the UMW; as late as 1897 the two unions were nearly identical
in size. From that time their paths diverged. The WFM
fought a series of celebrated but unsuccessful battles with
Western employers. By 1903 it was only one-tenth the size of
the UMW, a decade later only one-twentieth. In 1913 the
UMW called off merger talks because of the WFM's poor
prospects. On the eve of World War I, union density in the
Western hard-rock mining industry was no higher than in the
nation's factories.

The creation of the Central Competitive Field, the most
important and durable collective bargaining entity of the
pre–World War I years, was the basis for the UMW's remarkable growth. Beginning in 1898 operators and union representatives met annually to 1904, then biannually, to adjust wages
and address other labor issues. A joint wage scale committee
set interfield differentials to preserve competitive balance and
equalize earnings. The negotiations were often prolonged and
difficult; marathon sessions and strike threats were common.
Still, a commitment to industry stability overshadowed more
parochial concerns. The alternative, graphically illustrated at
Pana and Virden, Illinois, in 1898 and 1899, was a powerful
argument for cooperation. When the Illinois operators re-
neged on the 1898 scale and imported black strikebreakers,
the miners mobilized. The result was a series of battles that
degenerated into race riots, leaving at least eighteen dead and
dozens wounded. By the turn of the century the closed shop
and collective bargaining had become a formula for prosperity
and industrial peace in the Midwestern mining industry.

Having triumphed in the Midwest by demonstrating the
union's value to the industry, UMW leaders faced a different

but equally compelling challenge in the Eastern anthracite fields. The large number of "captive" mines (owned by transportation companies) and the supply of eastern European immigrant workers required new strategies. In the early 1890s Midwestern UMW officers had referred disparagingly to the anthracite fields as unorganizable. Yet when a UMW representative toured the area to raise money for the 1894 strike, he discovered widespread unrest. Several organizers followed, and by January 1895 there were more than fifty locals, with five thousand members. The depression reduced paid-up membership to two hundred in 1897, but the revival of the economy and the success of the Midwestern miners had a positive effect. So too did leadership changes within the UMW, notably the 1899 election of John Mitchell as president. Young, handsome, and conciliatory, Mitchell belied the popular image of the labor boss. If his relations with men like Ohio Senator Marcus Hanna (long a prominent force in operators' circles) and other moderate corporate executives were uncomfortably close, they nevertheless emphasized the breadth of his appeal.

One of Mitchell's first steps was to reorganize UMW operations in the anthracite region, creating a separate Wyoming (Pennsylvania) district and a role for Thomas D. Nicholls, the eighteen-year-old president of the new district. Under Nicholls's direction, the Wyoming district grew rapidly. Numerous local strikes generated interest and encouraged Mitchell to extend the scope of the anthracite campaign. A successful 1900 strike, involving all the anthracite fields for the first time since 1871, demonstrated the union's potential. At the end of the year the UMW had 53,000 members in anthracite, 29,000 of whom worked in the Wyoming mines.

These successes paved the way for the famous 1902 strike. Mitchell's shrewd leadership and contacts prompted the intervention of President Theodore Roosevelt and the creation of a

national commission to resolve the dispute. Unlike so many
earlier strikes, the 1902 conflict was peaceful; the most important events occurred in hearing rooms as the commission
weighed the charges and countercharges of the two sides. The
commission ultimately granted a wage increase but rejected
UMW demands for recognition and a dues checkoff. By
nineteenth-century standards it was a dramatic victory. The
UMW had waged a peaceful but successful strike, orches-
trated government intervention under favorable terms, and
emerged with an enhanced reputation and a larger membership. Few operators and fewer employees missed the significance of the anthracite settlement.

Hard-rock mine operators were among those most sensitive
to the growth of organized labor. They were as anti-union and
as pragmatic as the coal operators, but they differed in two important particulars. First, they were less interested in industry
stability because their economic outlook was healthier. Government price-fixing protected gold mining companies, and
the expansion of telephone and electric power service created
a positive environment for copper producers. Second, Western
operators had been more successful than Eastern coal operators in enlisting state and local governments as partisan forces
against the union. They had demonstrated the effectiveness of
such partnerships in the 1890s at Coeur d'Alene. After 1903
their value became unmistakable.

Employer resistance had been growing in Colorado since
the early 1890s, when a series of violent clashes at Cripple
Creek, Leadville, and Teluride turned most operators into implacable enemies of the WFM. In 1903 mine owners and managers formed the Citizens' Alliance of Denver and the State
Citizens' Alliance of Colorado, the most powerful and aggressive units of an emerging national open-shop movement.
They soon enlisted the new Republican governor, James H.

Peabody. With the governor's support, employers replaced pro-union local officials, arrested and deported strikers and other union members, and liberally used the militia to fight the WFM. The most famous incident in their campaign occurred at Cripple Creek in June 1903, when a bombing killed thirteen strikebreakers. In retaliation, the local employers' association forced the resignations of thirty pro-union public officials and mounted an assault on the union hall, killing and wounding a half-dozen men. The new sheriff rounded up union activists and deported anyone who refused to disavow the WFM. Within two days the WFM had been extinguished in Teller County, a union stronghold since the 1880s. The Colorado "war" of 1903–1904 was a dramatic demonstration of the WFM's vulnerability.

WFM leaders met similar problems when they began to organize Midwestern copper and iron miners. In 1906 the WFM mobilized disgruntled Finnish trammers in the Michigan mines, struck, and won a wage increase. The next year it led an unsuccessful strike of more than ten thousand Minnesota iron miners. The employers' ability to enlist thousands of strikebreakers at short notice was a critical factor in the outcome. In 1913 the Michigan locals again walked out, precipitating the most violent Midwestern conflict of the era. The operators relied on the now familiar formulas of strikebreakers, guards, appeals to public authorities, and legal action against the union. Although Michigan's governor refused to play the role of Colorado's Peabody, the National Guard kept the mines open and harassed union activists. Five participants died and a much larger number were wounded in clashes with guards. An anti-union mob kidnaped, beat, and deported WFM president Charles Moyer. Yet the most tragic event of the ten-month strike occurred after most of the now destitute strikers had returned to work. Calls of "fire" at a union Christmas party caused a stampede that left sixty-two children dead. This disaster was a symbolic turning point in the history of the WFM. Membership declined rapidly in the following years as employers routinely adopted the anti-union tactics honed in Colorado and Michigan.

James Foster's statistical analysis of the experiences of WFM locals helps explain the WFM's plight. His data suggests that neither big-business power nor WFM radicalism explains the union's decline. Large companies were no more anti-union than small firms and in some cases (in Butte, for example) were more tolerant and accommodating. By the same token, most local officials and miners were not socialists or revolutionaries. They preferred the AFL to the IWW and favored a merger with the UMW. Yet the WFM's reputation often deprived it of needed allies. As a result, Foster concludes, "only the large and tough unions proved too difficult for the mine corporations to break." But even they did not bring stability to labor-management relations. Missing from hard-rock industrial relations were the elaborate negotiations and agreements that characterized the Eastern coal fields. Collective bargaining provided the union with a recognized role in the industry and a mechanism for protecting workers against reprisals. Many new WFM locals collapsed because local leaders could not provide such elementary services or resorted to strikes in vain efforts to do so.

Despite their resources and commitment to collective bargaining, UMW leaders encountered many of the same problems when they shifted their sights from Pennsylvania and the Midwest to the unorganized fields. After 1902 they devoted more attention to central and southern West Virginia than to any other area. West Virginia's abundant, high-quality coal and poor workers made the area attractive to operators and a menace to the UMW. Organization would reduce or eliminate the operators' competitive advantage; preventing it therefore became essential to the state's interest. The result was an almost continuous conflict from the 1890s to World War I.

The most prolonged prewar conflict was the year-long Paint Creek–Cabin Creek strike of 1912–1913. Beginning in the spring of 1912, when the operators refused to renew a wage agreement, the conflict became a classic miners' strike, featuring evictions, strikebreakers, hired guards, tent colonies, shootings, and martial law. No one counted the casualties, though several incidents supposedly resulted in a dozen or more deaths. Private armies garrisoned the company towns, strikers terrorized strikebreakers, and each side engaged in military-style maneuvers. State authorities and National Guard units were not as partisan as their Colorado counterparts, but the practical difference was slight. By accepting the premise that their duty was to keep the mines open, they became de facto allies of the operators' forces. Amid much bitterness, the strike finally ended in a settlement that left the antagonists at loggerheads.

Bloody as the West Virginia battles were, none of them exceeded the brutality of a 1913–1914 UMW strike against Colorado Fuel and Iron. The issue was a union presence in Western coal and steel, since CFI mines provided fuel for the company's Pueblo steel operation. As the largest Colorado industrial firm, CFI had no trouble enlisting the Colorado government. In April 1914 National Guard forces and strikers met in a large-scale battle that became known as the Ludlow massacre. The casualties included combatants on both sides as well as thirteen women and children who perished when the soldiers attacked and burned their camp. Altogether at least seventy-four people died in the Colorado conflict, making it the worst single labor dispute of the pre–World War I years.

In spite of their victory, the CFI owners, the Rockefellers, were so chagrined that they expanded the company's welfare program and introduced a pioneering company union.

The conflicts of 1912–1914 marked a turning point in the development of the UMW. UMW leaders had taken advantage of the workers' desire for a formal voice, the instability of the industry, and the public's impatience with violence to create the nation's largest and most influential union. Their record contrasted markedly with that of the WFM, which by 1915 was a shadow of its former self. Yet even the UMW faced serious obstacles, notably on the industry's geographical periphery where anti-union employers employed the open shop as a competitive weapon. If the UMW suffered defeats or near defeats in West Virginia and Colorado, what hope was there for smaller and weaker organizations?

## EXPANSION AND REACTION

As the economy recovered in the late 1890s, the urban labor movement grew at a record pace. From 1897 to 1904, union membership rose from less than 500,000 to more than 2 million. In both absolute and relative terms, the 1904 total was a record. In 1898 New York had 87 cities and towns with at least one union; in 1903 it had 195. Michigan had 111 locals with 10,000 members in 1898; by 1903 there were 589 locals with 43,000 members. And while unions met greater opposition after 1904, gains more than offset losses; membership grew more slowly, but it continued to rise.

The principal effect of the boom was to strengthen organizations that were already relatively strong. Eighty-five percent of new members joined unions that had existed in 1897. The ten largest national unions accounted for nearly half the aggregate membership increase. Fifty-eight new national unions appeared between 1897 and 1904, but their aggregate membership in 1904 was only 236,000, or about 12 percent of the total. The Teamsters, formed in 1899, accounted for a third of it.

One other trend stood out. Unions of factory workers did not expand as rapidly as other unions, and most of their new members were employees of small, traditional factories. In 1897 the Cigarmakers, Molders, Machinists, and Typographical unions had been among the ten largest organizations. Seven years later only the Machinists retained that distinction. The Cigarmakers and Printers had reached the limits of their comparatively small jurisdictions. The metalworkers' organizations faced more formidable challenges. Many of their existing and potential members worked for firms that had merged into large new corporations. The employers now had greater resources than ever before, and some of them were devoted to welfare and personnel plans designed to reduce discontent. Others were used to defeat organizing campaigns. The limited successes of the Molders and Machinists, the continuing decline of the once formidable Iron and Steel Workers, and the near collapse of the Meat Cutters after a strike against the Chicago meat packers suggested the extent of the problem.

New or aspiring union leaders had two models of union organization to choose from. The first was the UMW, the best-known American labor organization. Despite its prominence, the UMW was an industrial union which reflected the distinctive conditions of the coal industry. The other choice was the United Brotherhood of Carpenters, the second largest union by 1904 and the most formidable building trades organization. Carpenters were also autonomous workers in an organizationally fragmented, unmechanized industry. Their work was highly seasonal. Yet they had little in common with miners.

Traditional carpentry was mastered only after years of instruction and on-the-job experience; it commanded high wages and social status. Mastery of the craft also opened the door to entrepreneurial opportunities. Skill and upward mobility shaped the perspective of the carpenters and their union leaders.

By the 1890s most Carpenters' locals had business agents who negotiated with employers, enforced agreements, and conducted the day-to-day affairs of the locals. In larger towns, where there was more than one local, district councils of business agents wielded power. Where several building trades unions operated, business agents formed building trades councils to coordinate local activities and add an element of industrial unionism to the prevailing craft structure. Many business agents were also active in local politics. In San Francisco, the most notable case, the building trades council dominated the city government for many years. To guide the national union, business agents created an administration party, not unlike the party machines they found at city hall. In president William D. Hutcheson, elected in 1915, the Carpenters had an aggressive representative of their interests.

Even before Hutcheson's rise, the Carpenters had redefined their jurisdiction. They recognized that high wages (their goal) encouraged technological innovation and the emergence of new, competitive occupations. In the early twentieth century their greatest challenges came from manufacturers of building components (doors, windows, trim) and substitute materials (steel in particular). The Carpenters' response was to recruit the most important workers in industries that competed with traditional carpenters. There were two milestones in this process. In 1911 they persuaded the AFL to recognize predominant unions in particular industries rather than narrow, occupationally based unions; and in 1913, after a long rivalry, they absorbed the Amalgamated Woodworkers, a union of factory workers. Carpenters admitted only about half the Woodworkers' members, those who performed strategically important tasks. This tactic enabled them to protect their core membership without opening their doors to laborers and other low-skill employees.

Where the UMW had succeeded by organizing mine employees regardless of occupation, the Carpenters scorned both industrial unionism and the elitist approach of the railroad brotherhoods. To their base of traditional skilled employees they added strategically important groups of less-skilled factory workers, becoming "craft-industrial." This approach enabled them to keep pace with technological change and served as a model for other unions. The economist Theodore Glocker reported in 1915 that there were only 28 pure craft unions and 5 industrial unions out of a total of 133 national unions. The other 100 were "of an intermediate type." By adopting a flexible, opportunistic approach, unions were able to achieve a degree of permanence unknown in the nineteenth century.

The Carpenters' other important contribution was to emphasize the value of order and system. The business agents understood the construction industry, their members' interests, and their place in the union. They operated as middle managers in an organization that was businesslike in its internal order and bureaucratic in the sense that well-defined procedures governed the actions of its leaders. They could be fiery and passionate if the occasion arose, but typically they scorned conflict as wasteful and dangerous.

This attitude, like the craft-industrial approach, became the standard of the labor movement in the years before World War I. In a sense it was a logical extension of the decision to organize nationally. But it was not inevitable; Peter McGuire and other established leaders fought it, and many contempo-

rary socialists and reformers, such as Ed Boyce and Charles
Moyer, rejected it. The decisive influences were external. The
rapidly escalating employer counterattack of the early twentieth century subjected union leaders to mounting pressures.
Weak organizations quickly succumbed. In this new and
more demanding setting, internal order and discipline were
essential to survival.

The employer offensive dated from a 1901 open-shop campaign in Dayton, Ohio. Unions had made rapid progress in
the city's industrial firms since 1897; by 1900 they could claim
ten thousand members and the ability to paralyze many firms.
Alarmed, employers organized and took the offensive. They
refused union demands, locked out union workers, and proclaimed the open shop. By 1902 the Dayton labor movement
was a fraction of its former size, and the open shop prevailed
in the city's industrial plants.

The Dayton experience provided the major ingredients of
local and national employer campaigns. First and foremost
was a counterorganization, modeled after the AFL's central
labor unions. By 1904 most cities had employers' associations
that coordinated anti-union activities, employed spies to report on union doings, and recruited strikebreakers. Some associations also operated employment agencies to screen job
applicants. Second was a propaganda campaign emphasizing
the unions' monopolistic intentions and unfairness to nonmembers. These appeals struck a responsive chord in a public
already anxious about monopolies. To many people a labor
monopoly was no different from a business monopoly. The
UMW had won the 1902 anthracite strike by successfully por-
traying itself as defender of the poor and downtrodden.
Within a few years it was almost impossible to repeat that feat,
largely because of the employers' propaganda.

In 1903 open-shop employers created a national organization to coordinate local and state activities and oppose union initiatives in the state legislatures and in Congress. The Citizens Industrial Association grew rapidly as the open-shop movement spread and employers persuaded themselves that a national open-shop organization was necessary. The association's influence peaked in 1908, then declined as employers realized that unions were addressed most effectively through individual effort, community organizations, or trade associations. The greatest achievement of the Citizens Industrial Association was to bring together a group of anti-union zealots who would remain active for a generation. The catalyst was David M. Parry, president of the National Association of Manufacturers (NAM). Parry guided the formation of the Citizens Industrial Association and presided over the conversion of the NAM into the most persistent opponent of the labor movement. Other anti-union professionals included Frederick W. Job, head of the highly successful Chicago Employers Association; Herbert George, an architect of the Colorado attack on the Western Federation of Miners; and Walter Drew, secretary of the National Erectors Association and the leader of a celebrated attack on the International Association of Bridge and Structural Iron Workers.

Apart from providing local services, the open-shop movement promoted legal assaults on union power. The NAM, the National Erectors Association, and the American Anti-Boycott Association, formed in 1902, were aggressive and effective litigants. Their successes in the courts helped make the legal injunction a favored employer tactic in strikes and other disputes. They also had a second, unintended effect that was more important in the short term: open-shop activities pushed the AFL into partisan politics in an unsuccessful effort to reform the antitrust laws and curb the use of injunctions. AFL leaders hoped to influence both parties, but when the Republi-

cans proved unresponsive, they moved into the Democratic
orbit.

## Organizing Factory Workers, 1904–1915

While unions generally made little progress in organizing
large or small manufacturing companies, a handful of exceptions stood out. By employing the UMW model—industrial
unionism combined with mass action—rather than the Carpenters' model, a few unions were able to attract large numbers of factory workers. Their experiences inspired many
activists, particularly those who were critical of the AFL and
the trend toward craft-industrial unionism. But they also emphasized the need for an aggressive, systematic strategy after
the initial phase of organization.

After its formation in 1905 as a mechanism for carrying the
WFM message of militant industrial unionism to workers
outside the mining industry, the Industrial Workers of the
World (IWW) had generated more conflict than union memberships. Beginning in 1909 it shifted its focus from Western
industry to the East in an effort to broaden its base and prove
that AFL unions were cautious to the point of negligence. The
IWW led a dozen major strikes and achieved even greater no-
toriety than it had in the West. Most of the conflicts started as
spontaneous walkouts over grievances; faced with the formidable task of managing a strike with little assistance from
local unions, strike leaders turned to the "Wobblies." IWW
leaders used mass action to unify the strikers and keep the employers on the defensive. IWW strikes at Lawrence, Massachusetts (1911–1912), Paterson, New Jersey (1913), and
Akron, Ohio (1913), were among the largest and best publicized of the era. Although the Lawrence strike produced the
only IWW victory, the Wobbly presence markedly prolonged

the others. The Wobblies were less successful at concluding strikes. Their hostility to formal negotiations and written contracts left successful strikers, such as those at Lawrence, vulnerable to piecemeal attack and deprived others of the prospect of negotiated concessions.

The best measure of what was possible was a series of dramatic strike victories between 1909 and 1913 by New York and Chicago clothing workers. By most measures the clothing workers were among the most downtrodden factory employees. Yet they also had several advantages. Most of them were Jewish immigrants from Russia, a background that inspired a shared sense of grievance and an interest in organization. The large number of women workers in the industry and the dominance of small firms and "chaotic" conditions also became unexpected sources of strength. The women's presence was instrumental in attracting outside support, and the multitude of small firms reduced the likelihood of a well-financed, unified opposition.

Four major strikes in New York and Chicago followed near-identical patterns. The first, involving more than 20,000 New York "shirtwaist" makers, mostly Jewish women, set the stage. The conflict began in September 1909 as a protest against low wages and poor working conditions. It spread rapidly, revitalizing the near-moribund International Ladies Garment Workers Union. The strikers enlisted influential outsiders, including prominent social workers, philanthropists, and members of the Women's Trade Union League. By February 1910 the union had concluded agreements with most of the shirtwaist manufacturers; more than 90 percent of them provided for the closed shop. Strikes of 50,000 New York cloak and suit workers in 1910, 40,000 men's clothing workers in Chicago in 1910–1911, and more than 100,000 men's clothing workers in New York in 1912–1913 brought

more victories and large union membership gains. In 1914 the
Chicago and New York men's clothing workers seceded from
the United Garment Workers and formed the Amalgamated
Clothing Workers. Sidney Hillman, the Chicago strike leader
and new Amalgamated president, committed the union to an
ambitious program of industry stabilization that bore many
similarities to John McBride's 1894 plan for the coal industry.

In the short term, however, the most important results of
the strikes were a series of elaborate collective bargaining
agreements. The 1910 conclusion to the cloak and suit workers' strike, the "Protocol of Peace," created a "government" to
oversee the industry's labor relations. The Chicago agreement
of 1911 provided for a similar mechanism, and later clothing
workers' contracts included various forms of arbitration. The
original protocol collapsed in 1914, but the protocol approach
was a major breakthrough. Not only did it provide a means of
resolving conflicts, it also created an important link between
the union and the workers. Union officials became as important to the workers as business agents were to construction
employees.

By 1915 the clothing workers unions had demonstrated that
manufacturing was not necessarily as different from mining
and construction as it had often seemed. They had organized
the kinds of workers that other union leaders dismissed as unorganizable, won closed-shop or preferential union-shop
agreements in New York, Chicago, and other centers, and
made themselves essential to the workers' progress. In the following years of war mobilization and government activism,
other unions would have novel opportunities to demonstrate
their value to their constituents and their industries.

## World War I and After, 1915–1930

From 1915 to 1922 union membership fluctuated more dramatically than at any time since the 1880s. Although the pattern of expansion and decline during those years was reminiscent of the boom-and-bust cycles of the nineteenth century, the period is better seen as a second phase of the expansion that began in 1897, with many of the same themes. Union membership grew substantially, and collective bargaining became more widespread than ever before. Employers remained overwhelmingly hostile, relying on legal and extralegal means to thwart organizers and sabotage unions. Manufacturing remained the principal battleground and the source of most of the variation in union membership. Indeed, apart from manufacturing, the pattern of these years is one of steadily increasing membership and growing union density.

The stimulus for these dramatic events was, of course, World War I. The war reduced the supply of new workers by ending European immigration to the United States; encouraged a boom in industrial production; and caused a dramatic expansion of the government's role in the economy. Government regulation of industry—hitherto a hotly contested issue—became more acceptable. All these effects contributed to the growth of the labor movement by reducing the employers' ability to punish employees for union activity. The war atmosphere also promoted the discussion of more radical goals, such as worker control of production and public ownership of industry. By creating a sense of ever-greater union power, these discussions may have persuaded some cautious workers to join the labor movement, particularly in industries such as steel, where union weakness had made employees vulnerable to reprisals. But the effect was brief and limited. Radicalism was the one sure way to unite opponents of union activity.

Union membership data provide a measure of the respective effects of the European war and American mobilization. The war began in August 1914 and by mid-1915 had a substantial impact on the U.S. labor force. American mobilization began in earnest after the declaration of war in April 1917 and grew extensive and effective the following spring. Through 1920 it continued to influence union activity. The following table reports the effects on union membership, by sector, from 1915 to 1920.

UNION MEMBERSHIP GROWTH, 1915–1920 (PERCENTAGE)

| Industry | 1915–1917 | 1917–1920 |
|---|---|---|
| Mining | 12 | 17 |
| Construction | 14 | 46 |
| Manufacturing | 24 | 97 |
| Transportation | 21 | 80 |
| Services | 5 | 27 |
| Miscellaneous* | 52 | 50 |
| All Industries | 16 | 65 |
| Annual Growth Rate | 8 | 18 |

*Mostly AFL federal labor unions, concentrated in manufacturing.

From 1904 to 1915, union membership grew at an average rate of 2 percent each year. The war quadrupled that rate, and mobilization produced a ninefold increase. The accelerated growth rates of 1917–1920, due largely to government policies that encouraged collective bargaining, resulted in approximately 1.2 million more union members. Between 1915 and 1920, government support accounted for about half the increase in union membership.

Although all industries experienced substantial increases in union membership, the most dramatic changes occurred in manufacturing and transportation, reflecting the wartime emphasis on industrial production. By simultaneously increasing the demand for industrial employees and reducing the supply, the war created bottlenecks in skilled labor markets and a general shortage of entry-level employees. Wages rose and turnover increased. Employers responded by recruiting native workers, including unconventional employees (married women and blacks, for example). Unions responded with aggressive recruiting efforts. Inflation, which wiped out most of the wage gains of 1915 and 1916, provided an additional incentive for organization. Most critical, however, was the workers' comparative immunity from reprisals. Many traditionally nonunion firms refused to recognize unions or sign contracts, but did not exclude union members: if they had, workers would simply have gone to more accommodating competitors. Many other employers bargained informally with their employees. The war economy thus permitted workers to consider a range of options. Approximately one-third of new employees between 1915 and 1917, including most coal miners, construction workers, and railroad employees, and a smaller percentage of factory workers, chose a formal voice.

This pattern continued after April 1917, but it was the pro-labor policies of the Wilson administration that produced the significant gains noted in the table above. Those policies reflected domestic politics as well as the exigencies of the war effort. Since 1908 the AFL and the Democratic party had been allies—the unions sought restrictions on the use of injunctions in labor disputes; minority Democrats sought additional votes. The results were negligible until 1916, when Congress passed the Adamson Act, establishing the eight-hour day as the standard for the railroad industry, and several lesser AFL-backed measures. The outbreak of war brought still greater benefits. Wilson appointed Samuel Gompers to his chief advisory group and established a series of tripartite boards (employers, representatives of organized labor, and "public" members) to address labor problems in defense industries. Although the employers and public members often outvoted the union members, the inclusion of union representatives made an aggressively anti-union policy impossible. Coupled with the labor shortage, this approach effectively opened the door to union organizers.

To the Carpenters and their strong-minded president, William D. Hutcheson, this imprecise but permissive policy was unsatisfactory. In 1917 and early 1918 Hutcheson battled several mobilization agencies over their refusal to embrace the closed shop. His conflict with the tripartite board for the shipbuilding industry led to mounting criticism of the union and the labor movement. Ultimately it defined the limits of the administration's pro-union policy. As long as unions remained cooperative, sensitive to public opinion, and supportive of the war effort, they could expect a free hand in exploiting an advantageous situation. Inflexibility or political dissent, on the other hand, were unacceptable.

The premier example of government-labor cooperation was the railroad industry after mounting congestion in late 1917 led to a government takeover. To improve morale and avoid disputes, the U.S. Railroad Administration granted workers a larger voice in railroad operations. The brotherhoods responded enthusiastically; by 1919 they were so pleased with the new arrangements that they abandoned their traditional conservatism for the Plumb Plan, which called for continued government ownership and a large union role in policymaking. The Railroad Administration also permitted nonoperating employees to organize, contrary to the policies of most railroads. This policy represented a major change.

Unions such as the Railroad Telegraphers, Maintenance of Way Employees, Station Employees, and Railroad Clerks enjoyed an unprecedented boom. The Boilermakers, Machinists, and other metal trades organizations also recruited tens of thousands of shopcraft employees.

In the case of defense contractors, government policy was less clear and consistent, at least until the 1918 formation of the National War Labor Board. At one extreme was the Chicago meat packing industry, since 1904 an open-shop bastion. In 1917 the Amalgamated Meat Cutters and other unions formed a Stockyards Labor Council to organize the packinghouses. Membership grew rapidly, and the unions gained various concessions, though not formal recognition. Negotiations deadlocked in early 1918, and the packers reluctantly agreed to arbitration. In March the arbitrator, a federal judge, endorsed union demands for an eight-hour day and a substantial wage increase. The union victory encouraged other workers to join. By the end of the war the Chicago plants were almost completely organized. In earlier years this would have been a remarkable development given the prevalence of low-skill workers.

At the other extreme were unions that did not support the war effort. The most notable example was the IWW, which in 1917 and 1918 won a renewed following in the Rocky Mountain West. From Arizona to Washington, employers took the offensive, often with the active encouragement and assistance of federal authorities. Using tactics reminiscent of the Coeur d'Alene conflicts of the 1890s and the Colorado labor war of 1903–1905, they ruthlessly suppressed IWW activity. In Bisbee, Arizona, they deported more than a thousand suspected Wobblies and other miners; in the Pacific Northwest, employers and military officers created the Loyal Legion of Loggers and Lumbermen to exclude the IWW from logging camps. In Butte a mob lynched IWW organizer Frank Little. The indictment of virtually all Wobbly leaders in September 1917 for interfering with the war effort emphasized the government's role in the anti-union campaign.

In the spring of 1918 the Wilson administration created the National War Labor Board to bring order or at least consistency to federal labor policy. Although limited to war industries that did not have a specific tripartite board, the NWLB made rapid progress. Under Frank Walsh, the pro-union cochairman who dominated the board, the NWLB promoted collective bargaining as an antidote to unrest and conflict. This policy did not require recognition of an outside union; most firms in fact satisfied the board's demands by creating company unions. Yet the board's endorsement of union methods helped maintain a positive environment for organization. Unions could boast to prospective members that the government was on their side.

From the union perspective, the only problem with the NWLB and other wartime agencies was their brief duration. The armistice in November 1918 was followed by a rapid demobilization that eliminated most ad hoc administrative agencies, including the tripartite boards. In early 1919 the NWLB simply stopped functioning. The exceptions were the Railroad Administration and the meat packing industry plan, which did not depend on the mobilization authority. Workers outside these industries soon concluded that strikes were the only way to win their demands. The number of strikes in 1919 set a record that survived until the mid-1930s.

In fact the postwar situation was even less favorable than this summary suggests. Wilson's preoccupation with the Versailles treaty and his later physical collapse left domestic affairs in the hands of conservative administrators who had little sympathy for workers or the AFL-Democratic alliance. Attorney General A. Mitchell Palmer's crusade against political radicals symbolized this shift. At the same time the decline in government spending, coupled with a more restrictive Federal Reserve policy, brought the wartime boom to an end. In the fall of 1920 mass layoffs began. By early 1921 none of the conditions that had encouraged union growth remained. Still, after five years of unprecedented growth, the labor movement was powerful, confident, and militant. Would its enhanced position enable it to survive the postwar return to "normalcy"?

### A Lost Decade, 1920–1930?

The following table provides a partial answer to the question of union vitality. Membership fell precipitously during the early twenties, wiping out most of the gains of the mobilization period. Unions of factory workers (including the shopcraft employees) suffered the greatest losses, followed by the railroad organizations and others. (The UMW briefly increased its membership before declining rapidly in the mid- and late 1920s.) These were predictable losses. The unpredictable part of the postwar story was the relatively poor performance of the labor movement in the years after 1923, when the economy grew rapidly and employment and real wages rose. Continuing losses under such conditions led many observers to suspect that the problem was deeper than the new conservative political order. They charged that the statistics reflected AFL complacency, lethargy, and misguided policies, as well as the less friendly political environment. Their indictment became an important feature of most histories of the period.

UNION MEMBERSHIP GROWTH, 1920–1929 (PERCENTAGE)

| Industry | 1920–1923 | 1923–1929 |
|---|---|---|
| Mining | 21 | -49 |
| Construction | -11 | 16 |
| Manufacturing | -51 | -15 |
| Transportation | -28 | -1 |
| Services | 0 | 46 |
| Miscellaneous* | -57 | 0 |
| All Industries | -28 | -5 |
| Annual Rate of Change | -10 | -1 |

*Mostly AFL federal labor unions, concentrated in manufacturing.

Whatever the deficiencies of the AFL or of individual unions, they had only a modest effect on union membership. The postwar experience of American unions was not comparable to either the late nineteenth century (rapid growth followed by precipitous decline) or the late twentieth century (long-term decline). Rather, unions quickly adjusted to a more demanding environment. Three points stand out. First, though aggregate membership fell after 1920, the total never declined below the level of 1917, which had been a record high at the time. Even in 1929 the labor movement was more than 10 percent larger than it had been in 1917. Nor did any major union disappear. Well managed or not, unions had achieved a degree of organizational stability that would have been unimaginable a half-century before.

Second, as noted in this table, the most devastating losses occurred in manufacturing. Some were due to declining employment and some, as in steel and meat packing, to union defeats in 1919 and 1921 respectively. In view of the prewar record of unions in manufacturing, some setbacks were almost inevitable. Employers aimed their postwar open-shop campaign, based on the so-called "American Plan," at factory workers. By 1929 union members in manufacturing were mostly autonomous workers employed in small firms. Organization in mass-production industries was negligible, as it had been in 1915. The difference was that many conventional union leaders now believed, as a result of their wartime experiences, that such industries *could* be organized. Even the AFL, realistic to a fault, financed an ambitious and ultimately unsuccessful 1929 campaign in Southern textiles. The ghost of war mobilization persisted.

Third, some unions continued to prosper. By 1929 the building trades organizations had thirty thousand more members than they had had at their wartime peak. The Carpenters, Bricklayers, Painters, and Sheet Metal workers grew slowly, but during the 1920s the lowly Hod Carriers nearly tripled its membership. Many service-sector unions, led by the musicians and federal government employees' organizations, also grew. Together with the railroad brotherhoods, streetcar workers, and Teamsters, they provide an alternative to portrayals of decline based on manufacturing.

The experiences of railroad workers summarize several tends of the postwar era. Over the objections of the unions, Congress in 1920 passed the Transportation Act, creating the Railroad Labor Board. The board's effort to reduce wages led to the 1922 strike. Meanwhile the brotherhoods, led by the customarily apolitical BLE, launched a campaign against the board that led to support for the third-party presidential campaign of Robert La Follette in 1924 and ultimately to sponsorship of the Howell-Barkley Bill, the basis of the 1926 Railroad Labor Act. This act created a board more amenable to union influence, virtually guaranteed collective bargaining for organized employees, and provided a precedent for other regulatory measures. The beneficiaries of this activity were the

brotherhoods, especially the well-established unions of engineers, firemen, trainmen, and conductors. The shopcraft
unions received little assistance. The clerks, maintenance-of-
way workers, and signalmen also declined when employers,
having defeated the shopworkers, turned their attention to
other nonoperating employees.

The most remarkable development of the decade, and the
single most important contribution to the perception of union
decline, was the virtual collapse of the UMW. At the end of
the war the UMW had been more powerful than ever; it had a
major voice in the Fuel Administration, could count on the
support of virtually all Northern miners, and boasted a large
corps of experienced, aggressive leaders. It suffered minor
losses during the postwar recession but after 1924 faced more
serious problems. By 1929 membership had fallen to the level
of 1911, with no prospect of revival. UMW losses accounted
for the decline in aggregate union membership. The fate of
the UMW cast a pall over the labor movement.

Despite its strength, the postwar UMW faced the same
dilemma that had haunted its nineteenth-century predecessors. If it did not recruit every new miner, its strength would
erode. As it approached its goal and labor costs rose, it created
powerful incentives for nonunion operators to open new
mines. During the war, with demand rising and coal prices at
record levels, the temptation became overwhelming. New
mines appeared throughout southern Appalachia and other
unorganized or lightly organized fields. When the UMW sent
organizers to these areas and tried to recruit members and
win contracts, the operators responded with strikebreakers,
guards, and wholesale evictions. The UMW campaign lasted
more than two years and featured a level of violence reminiscent of the most desperate earlier struggles. The battle of Mat-
tewan in May 1920 and the union assault at Blair Mountain in

1921 (part of the miners' "march" on Logan County, West Virginia) became legends. Dozens of miners and guards died, but in the end state and federal government intervention, ostensibly to preserve law and order, doomed the UMW effort. The failure of the West Virginia campaign encouraged more low-wage Southern operations. By 1929 UMW membership in West Virginia was negligible, and Southern coal dominated the bituminous market.

The decline of the coal industry in the 1920s exacerbated the impact of these setbacks. Growing competition from fuel oil and gasoline reduced the demand for bituminous coal, leaving the industry with excess capacity. Many mines operated sporadically, and thousands of miners worked part-time. A successful strike in one field simply created more work in other fields. Except in the anthracite fields, per capita earnings fell throughout the decade.

Severe as these problems were, they were not unique or insoluble. With slight variations they were the same problems the founders of the UMW had faced. In response, McBride and the others had organized aggressively and tried to convince employers of the union's value as a stabilizing force. What made the UMW less effective in the 1920s? A critical factor was the internal turmoil that consumed the organization. A leadership crisis might not have been so devastating a decade earlier or later, but now it came at a time of extreme vulnerability. The UMW was increasingly self-absorbed and unresponsive at a time when the industry's traditional problems demanded more, not less, attention.

The union's internal problems were closely associated with the rise of John L. Lewis, who in 1919 became president of the UMW. A shrewd tactician, able negotiator, and ruthless dictator, Lewis immediately made his mark. Among his contemporaries he most closely resembled William Hutcheson, the

equally imperious president of the Carpenters. Yet where
Hutcheson was unattractive and aloof, Lewis was an actor
who loved the public stage. He also involved himself in every
aspect of union operations. As a result the UMW, which was
relatively decentralized before Lewis's presidency, became increasingly centralized, with more and more appointed leaders
responsible to Lewis alone. Regional leaders did not surrender
without a struggle, and Lewis's battles with them were important landmarks of the transformation of the UMW. But by the
end of the decade these conflicts had eliminated many of the
ablest leaders and absorbed the energies of those who remained. The struggle with the operators often took a back
seat to the miners' own civil war.

Lewis's approach to the industry accelerated the union's decline. In the critical negotiations of 1922 and 1924 he vigorously fought wage reductions, not unlike many other union
leaders. But given the miners' weakness (and the graphic example of the shopcraft workers' fate), this strategy could only
spell disaster. Earlier UMW leaders had been flexible and accommodating until they had sufficient strength to make cred-
ible demands; Lewis was not. His insistence on unrealistic
wartime rates encouraged mine closings in the Central Competitive Field. By the late 1920s he began to emphasize a point
he would later push more vigorously: the desirability of eliminating some miners so the rest could demand higher wages.
By the late 1920s he had essentially written off the older
Northern fields.

The decline of the UMW was an important exception to the
pattern of union growth that dated from the recovery of 1897.
Yet even it could not obscure the most important development
of the first three decades of the new century: the close relationship between union strength and a pro-union public policy.

This lesson, more than the employers' ability to resist union encroachments or the difficulty of enlisting factory workers, stood out at the end of the decade. It would become even more compelling in the following years, as economic collapse and mass unemployment evoked memories of the 1890s and eroded the foundations of even the strongest unions.

# 5

# The Labor Movement at
# High Tide, 1930–1953

FROM A LOW of 3 million members in 1933, at the trough of the Great Depression, union membership grew to 5.8 million in 1938, 12 million in 1945, and 16.9 million in 1953. From 10 percent of the nonagricultural labor force in 1930, it rose to 35 percent in 1945 and 32 percent in the early 1950s. For most unions this growth was cumulative; except in 1937–1938 and 1945–1946, when a severe recession and the end of World War II precipitated mass layoffs, gains continually outnumbered losses.

The revival began in 1933–1936, as economic recovery increased employment opportunities, weakened employer resistance to union activity, and encouraged workers to take advantage of the favorable political environment. Mobilization for World War II (1941–1945) and the Korean War (1950–1953) strongly reinforced the peacetime pattern. The most important difference between these periods and the mid-1880s and late 1890s was the role of government, which now contributed to union growth. Not only did it help revive the miners' organizations, it enabled miners and others to use mass action to enlist large numbers of factory workers into seemingly permanent industrial unions. By 1953 a greatly expanded and strengthened labor movement could look to the future with confidence.

## PERSPECTIVE: 1937

Unlike the union revival of the late 1890s, the revival of the 1930s was front-page news. New leaders and organizations, dramatic confrontations, novel protest techniques, and, above all, a sense of activism seemed to mark these years as the beginning of a new era. Labor journalist Edward Levinson captured this perspective in the title of his 1938 book, *Labor on the March*. Better still was an event that Levinson featured, the great 1937 General Motors strike. The conflict had a David and Goliath character: General Motors was the world's largest and richest industrial corporation, a bastion of the open shop, and a premier example of the type of firm that had successfully resisted organization. The United Automobile Workers (UAW) was new and untested, and, unlike most successful twentieth-century unions, devoid of resources. Yet the strikers overcame potentially fatal setbacks and ultimately succeeded in wresting a modest contract from the company. Employers were startled. If a union such as the UAW could defeat General Motors, was any employer immune? The General Motors strike sent shock waves through the business world, though the reasons for the UAW triumph were more complex than most observers realized.

On the eve of the strike the UAW, like so many factory workers' organizations of earlier years, seemed headed for oblivion. The economic revival of 1933 and the passage of the National Industrial Recovery Act had spurred a wave of union organization in the auto industry. By the fall of 1933 there were numerous federal labor unions affiliated with the AFL; several independent unions, including a potentially powerful organization of tool and die workers; and many company unions. During the following year the federal locals and independent unions flourished while the company unions quickly declined. But company resistance also hardened, and the unions were unable to deliver the benefits they had promised. By the time the AFL chartered the UAW in mid-1935, most auto workers had become disillusioned. The refusal of employers to comply with the new Wagner Act and the government's inability to enforce the law created additional obstacles. Finally, the UAW itself was beset with internal problems: a weak and erratic president, rampant factionalism, and political infighting. How could a union with so many problems successfully confront a large corporation such as General Motors?

Despite these shortcomings, the UAW had two critical assets. It remained the only viable, independent workers' voice in the industry, and it had the potential support of an increasingly pro-union Roosevelt administration and a sympathetic Michigan governor, Frank Murphy, elected in the 1936 New Deal landslide. The critical test began in late 1936 with the arrival of the sit-down strike, an innovative form of mass action which had been widely used in Akron tire plants. The similarities between the tire and auto industries were obvious; by mid-1936 anyone could have foreseen the spread of the sit-down to the auto plants. UAW leaders simply took advantage of what would have happened with or without their encouragement. After that, other opportunities emerged.

UAW efforts to organize GM centered on the huge complex of parts, body, and assembly plants in Flint, Michigan. In 1935 the Flint local, like most UAW locals, had virtually collapsed. In mid-1936 Wyndam Mortimer, a UAW vice-president, attempted unsuccessfully to revive it. His successor, Bob Travis, managed to enlist a small but active group in

Fisher Body Plant 1, which would be the center of the strike. This group conducted a successful sit-down on November 13, winning concessions from the plant manager. Their victory, coupled with sit-downs in other auto plants in November and December, revived the labor movement in Flint and provided workers and union leaders with a clear idea of how to achieve their goals. Union membership grew rapidly in December, and a sense of impending confrontation revived the atmosphere of the early NRA period. Using the company's attempt to move machinery from one of the Flint plants as a pretext, on December 30 Travis ordered a sit-down. Workers in Fisher Body Plants 1 and 2 successfully occupied those facilities, bringing production to a halt and beginning the longest and most famous of all the sit-downs. GM workers in other cities followed the lead of the Flint strikers, staging sit-downs and conventional strikes. By the second week of January 1937, GM had been shut down. It remained shut, and in the case of the Flint plants occupied, for more than a month.

The UAW faced all the problems of conventional strikes plus the headaches of sustaining the sit-down strikers. It had no trouble raising sufficient funds from other locals and unions to support the strikers. It also received valuable assistance from the new Committee on Industrial Organization ("Committee" became "Congress" in 1938, when it was expelled from the AFL), which sent experts to manage the strikers' publicity and public relations. Nonstriking Flint-area UAW members and their families were equally helpful. The local's women's auxiliary and a paramilitary group within the auxiliary, the Women's Emergency Brigade, provided various services, from food preparation to picket duty.

The union's most obvious challenges were logistical. It had to provide food and other supplies to the strikers and sustain their enthusiasm through long periods of inactivity. Strike leaders formed quasi-military organizations in the plants, with regularly scheduled activities, individual job assignments, and calisthenics. Musical programs, dramas, and other forms of entertainment provided diversions. Although few, if any, of the strikers remained in the plants for the entire conflict, morale gradually declined. Poor living conditions and pressures from wives (no women were allowed to remain in the occupied plants) discouraged many of the strikers. Morale was relatively high in Plant 1, which employed younger men and had easier access to the outside; lower in Plant 2, which had an older, mostly married labor force; and poor in Plant 4, which was isolated and hard to supply.

Other challenges arose from efforts to break the strike. Most GM workers were either hostile or indifferent to the strike, and Flint's city officials and influential citizens were strongly opposed. Alone or together they constituted a serious threat. The Flint Alliance, formed on January 7 by nonstriking workers and local merchants, was potentially a strikebreaking force. In Anderson, Indiana, another GM town, nonstrikers drove out strike leaders and ransacked the local's headquarters. In Flint the city administration took the lead. On January 11 the police tried to enter the occupied plants, precipitating the "Battle of the Running Bulls," the most famous incident of the conflict. Stopped by a fusillade of car parts and ice water, the police responded with tear gas and bullets. They finally withdrew, but their attack achieved one of the mayor's objectives: it persuaded the governor to send the National Guard to Flint.

GM was a more formidable threat. Fortunately for the UAW, it proved no more adept at defending its interests than Flint's city fathers. The GM managers' goals were to force the evacuation of the plants and turn the strike into a conventional conflict which the side with superior resources, namely

GM, would win. The company controlled access to the plants. On two occasions when it cut off heat and light (once at the instigation of Governor Murphy), it created a crisis that would have forced an evacuation. In both cases, however, GM backed down. Supposedly company officials were worried about damage to the factories. But at least as important was their expectation that legal action would end the sit-down and label the strikers as lawbreakers. GM obtained an injunction against the strikers during the first week of the conflict, though it did not pressure the police to enforce it for another month. Nevertheless this tactic caused the company to hesitate at critical moments. By leaving the strikers in control of the plants, General Motors allowed the union to portray itself as David in deadly battle with a powerful but ineffectual Goliath.

For a firm such as GM to stumble so badly suggested more fundamental problems. GM executives were divided into two camps, headed respectively by operations vice-president William Knudsen and financial vice-president Donaldson Brown. Knudsen, who ultimately prevailed, advocated accommodations to end the conflict. Brown was more concerned about the long-term implications of a union presence. The extent of their differences is uncertain, but it may have prevented decisive leadership at critical times. In any case, the company's vascillating approach permitted the union to retain the initiative. In the end GM's indecision had as much to do with the outcome of the strike as the union's bold moves. General Motors had rarely made such mistakes in the past and would rarely make them after 1937.

Given the stalemate that continued through January and early February, it was ultimately the politicians, especially Governor Murphy, who determined the outcome. Murphy was committed to industrial peace and law and order. He advocated a negotiated solution, which implied something less than a union defeat. In mid-January he worked out an agreement for the evacuation of the plants, only to see it collapse when Knudsen announced that he would also negotiate with the Flint Alliance. Murphy continued to work for disengagement and negotiations, though his most important contribution was probably to assure union leaders that the National Guard would not be used to break the strike. After the strikers demonstrated their strength by seizing Plant 4 on February 3, he was instrumental in the final negotiations. Other politicians, including President Roosevelt and Secretary of Labor Frances Perkins, contributed to this result by publicizing the strike and preventing Anderson-style mob action against the union.

In the end GM conceded relatively little. It agreed to negotiate with the union and not to negotiate with other entities in seventeen plants, including the Flint plants, for six months. This was a deal that Knudsen and the production executives could live with. It meant only modest changes in day-to-day policies and freed them from the specter of continued sit-downs. They retained their powers on the shop floor and wielded those powers more shrewdly than they had managed the strike, effectively containing the UAW. Not until 1939, when Walter Reuther led a successful conventional strike of GM tool and die makers, did the union's fortunes improve. As late as 1940 it could claim only 14 percent of GM's production employees.

Still, the General Motors strike was more than a contest over power and resources. As everyone (except perhaps Knudsen) realized, it was also a struggle for legitimacy. By winning some concessions, the UAW achieved what few unions, and even fewer industrial unions, had achieved in American factories. It also sustained the mid-1930s image of labor dynamism in new and more favorable setting. Defeat might not have been a blow for the labor movement; other unions in other industries were equally active, and the disastrous Little Steel strike just three months later did not deter them. But defeat in Flint would have set back the UAW for several years and deepened the internal divisions that in 1938 nearly destroyed the union. It surely would have dissuaded many GM workers from thinking they could join a union without fear of reprisal. By avoiding defeat, the UAW set itself apart from a long tradition of failure and recrimination, and signaled the arrival of a new age.

## FOUNDATIONS OF A NEW ERA, 1933–1938

The depression of the 1930s and the New Deal inaugurated the single most important chapter in the history of the labor movement. After four years of continuous decline from 1928 to 1932, which reduced union density to its 1903 level, organized labor experienced a dramatic revival; by 1937 unions had added more than 2 million new members and density had risen to 1920 levels. The sudden expansion produced internal tensions and divisions that culminated in the formation in 1938 of a dual federation, the Congress of Industrial Organizations (CIO). The most remarkable feature of union growth in the 1930s, however, was the prominent role of factory workers and especially workers from the largest and most prominent factories. For the first time unions were able to attract industrial employees who had little or no autonomy and retain their support for extended periods. This achievement underlined the other major development of the 1930s, the expanded role of government in the economy. No one doubted that the organization of factory workers (and others) was a direct result of an activist, prolabor government.

The seriousness of the depression is apparent from union membership data. By 1933 construction workers' organizations had lost 37 percent of their 1930 members; railroad workers' unions 32 percent; and unions of manufacturing employees, already reduced to highly skilled employees, 14 percent. Service workers unions grew slightly, thanks to an increase in representation among federal government employees. Beset with internal strife, the UMW lost another 15 percent of its members. (If only working, dues-paying members had been counted, the toll would have been much higher.) The losers were no longer the unions most vulnerable to employer attack. Indeed, the healthiest unions of the 1920s suffered the greatest declines.

Led by the AFL, union executives joined the growing throng that demanded government initiatives to stimulate economic activity and create jobs. AFL leaders lobbied for shorter hours; Sidney Hillman, John L. Lewis, and other less orthodox union executives proposed sweeping plans that affected business as well as labor. They became part of the heterogeneous lobby that ultimately produced the National Industrial Recovery Act and the National Recovery Administration, the principal New Deal recovery agency. The NIRA authorized "codes and fair competition," or legalized cartels, which were supposed to improve business confidence, raise prices, and increase employment. In return for these concessions, employers had to acknowledge their employees' right to bargain collectively and observe certain minimum labor standards. These reforms were included in the NIRA's famous Section 7a, which attracted little attention in the drafting of the legislation or even in the specific code negotiations. The crisis atmosphere of early 1933 accounted for this remarkable oversight. To many business and political leaders, the depression was a national catastrophe, requiring sacrifice and cooperation. More cynical observers noted that Section 7a was more a pious hope than a precise requirement. The meaning of collective bargaining was open to interpretation, and the codes did not include an effective enforcement mechanism.

Whatever the reason, most employers grossly underestimated the potential of Section 7a. For the next year union organizers could argue that government *and* business endorsed collective bargaining. Employers who opposed unions had to explain why they had agreed to the codes. Finally, though the enforcement mechanism was deficient, NRA authorities had one useful resource, the power to publicize wrongdoing. To small firms in out-of-the-way places, this threat was meaningless. To more visible big businesses, it was potentially disastrous. Their reputations had been sullied by the depression, and negative publicity would only invite more trouble. Regardless of legalities, Section 7a required a new delicacy in employer-employee relations.

Industrial workers quickly realized they had a unique opportunity. Unions reported more than 600,000 new members in 1933, the largest increase since 1919. In many Northern cities prospective members had to wait in long lines to pay initiation fees. Some workers created their own unions, such as the Independent Union of All Workers in Austin, Minnesota, but the majority joined established unions. Workers in every occupation—from miners to factory workers to store clerks—organized, but two groups stood out. First were workers who had a history of organization. Notable examples were coal miners and clothing workers, who swelled their respective organizations. Second were skilled or strategically important workers who had considerable autonomy and were hard to replace. In the auto industry, for example, tool and die makers, body-plant workers, and employees of small and mid-sized manufacturers, vulnerable to strikes, took the lead.

While the activity and excitement of the spring and summer of 1933 were novel, the pattern of organization was almost identical to earlier periods.

The best example of this continuity was the miraculous resurgence of the United Mine Workers. After a decade of decline, the UMW was bereft of leaders and members. Lewis's policy of rule or ruin had left him as absolute ruler of a bankrupt empire. But he, better than anyone else, saw the potential of the NIRA. The passage of the act produced a spontaneous groundswell of activity; by July 1933 the UMW had enlisted thousands of its former members. Deftly using the workers' pent-up anger as a club over the operators and the Roosevelt administration, Lewis obtained a code that included something the UMW had never achieved on its own: a single agreement for the Northern and Southern soft-coal industries. Although wage differentials remained, the union received a dues checkoff, tantamount to a union shop. In the spring of 1934 Lewis completed his coup. He negotiated an agreement with the Appalachian operators that reduced the regional differentials and established the union shop in most bituminous fields. In less than a year Lewis had revived the UMW and made it stronger than ever before.

The reemergence of the UMW had broad significance for the labor movement. Now it was not only the nation's largest union but an extension of Lewis's personality and interests. He decided who rose or fell, who mattered and who did not. His power was again as great as that of other AFL stalwarts, but with a difference. While William Hutcheson and other veteran presidents focused on their own bailiwicks, Lewis had larger ambitions. With the UMW treasury at his disposal, he was ready for more expansive projects.

Except for the clothing workers' unions, which also remained under their leaders' firm control, Lewis's experience

was atypical. In most industries rapid growth created challenges, even crises. New members demanded services and expected immediate benefits. Having concluded that reprisals
were unlikely, they were ready to strike if higher wages and
better working conditions were not forthcoming. And they
had little patience with leaders who did not share their militancy or their optimism.

After a decade of stable or declining membership, experienced and proven union executives were in short supply.
Unions scrambled to fill the leadership vacuum. Individuals
who had been discarded in the earlier years suddenly found
their services in demand. Lewis, for example, turned to John
Broply, Powers Hapgood, and Adolph Germer, idealistic enemies who in the 1920s had fought him. AFL President
William Green enlisted William Collins and Francis Dillon to
preside over the unruly auto workers' locals and the equally
undistinguished Coleman Claherty to lead the equally unruly
rubber workers. All of them were quickly overwhelmed by
their responsibilities. Other leaders came from leftist groups
that had operated at the periphery of the labor movement
since the great World War I organizing campaigns. The
Communist Trade Union Unity League, the Socialist party,
and the Brookwood Labor College of Katonah, New York,
supplied numerous activists. By the summer of 1933 most of
them had achieved important positions.

Several examples illustrate this phenomenon. In New York
the Communist party had tried unsuccessfully in the early
1930s to organize transit workers. Then the NIRA embold-
ened the workers and encouraged Irish political activists to organize their coworkers, also disproportionately Irish. The
Communist and Irish groups soon coalesced. The Communists provided behind-the-scenes advice and support for the
new Transport Workers Union. They also recruited many

union officers into the party, though the rank-and-file members were 98 to 99 percent non-Communist. A similar process made the United Electrical Workers the largest Communist-dominated union. On the West Coast, members of the Communist Marine Workers Industrial Union dominated the International Longshoremen's and Warehousemen's Union. In the Detroit area many socialists, Communists, and other radicals achieved leadership positions in the auto workers' locals. Their internecine conflicts contributed to the UAW's chaotic internal affairs.

Regardless of background or perspective, union leaders faced a growing employer backlash in the spring of 1934. As the economy improved and the NRA became increasingly ineffectual, more and more employers spurned the recovery effort. No new national open-shop organizations appeared, though the National Association of Manufacturers and many local employers' associations became more active. Antiunionism in the 1930s was private and secretive. In small towns, where employers could count on local support, they routinely fired union activists. The disastrous conclusion to the great Southern textile workers' strike of 1934 was a dramatic example of a process that was occurring in hundreds of communities. In larger cities employers were more circumspect. They usually agreed to meet union representatives but rejected formal recognition, a contract, or anything that would imply a permanent relationship. They also set up company unions to wean workers from outside organizations. Their tactics made 1934 a record year for strikes—nearly 1,900 involving 1.5 million workers, with most newly organized unions either failing or winning only modest concessions. More delays and defeats in 1935, coupled with the collapse of the NRA, reversed the pattern of 1933. Members abandoned unions en masse, leaving the new organizations with a fraction of their 1934 membership.

As a consequence the labor movement of 1935 looked much like the labor movement of 1915 or 1925. With the exception of the building trades, which continued to struggle with depressed conditions, the most successful unions were organizations of autonomous industrial workers and service employees. The largest union was again the UMW. Skilled industrial workers' unions, such as the machinists, printers, and railroad organizations, also flourished. Otherwise the fastest-growing unions were service-sector organizations of musicians, waiters, truck drivers, and federal government employees. After 1934, organizations of low-skill factory workers, including the Amalgamated Clothing Workers and the ILGWU, suffered serious setbacks. The UAW and the Rubber Workers, whose formation had exacerbated tensions within the AFL and contributed to the formation of the CIO, were no larger than the Horseshoers or the Siderographers.

Yet this picture of the labor movement omits the dynamic forces that had a marked effect in the following years. The most important of these was the Wagner Act, passed in May 1935, which revived the collective bargaining guarantee of Section 7a, banned many of the tactics that employers had used to undermine it, and created a permanent National Labor Relations Board with enforcement powers. The Wagner Act had little obvious effect until the Supreme Court confirmed its constitutionality in April 1937; before then most employers simply dismissed it as unconstitutional and continued to reject union demands.

A second development was the emergence of the sit-down strike as a protest technique. The sit-down had entered American industrial life in June 1934, when frustrated union members at the General Tire Company in Akron, Ohio, used it to emphasize their demands for recognition. It reemerged in the fall of 1935 as tire workers protested against uncooperative employers and seemingly ineffectual unions. The most serious incidents occurred at the Goodyear Tire & Rubber Company. After several months of conflict over the company's effort to lengthen the workday, a group of union stewards and their followers, including nonunion employees, staged sit-downs to protest the company's actions. The sit-downs quickly escalated into a union-led conventional strike that closed the Goodyear plants in January and February 1936 and attracted wide attention. Rank-and-file workers, including nonunion workers, took the initiative; the union followed opportunistically; and together they won an unprecedented agreement from a major corporation that had long championed the open shop. The Goodyear strike created an appealing image of aggrieved workers shaping their own future.

A third dynamic was the emergence of the CIO, a self-appointed group of industrial unionists within the AFL. John L. Lewis formed the CIO and remained its leader: his personality and UMW bank account gave it visibility and legitimacy. The CIO sought to encourage organization in large-scale manufacturing. Lewis naturally attracted the leaders of the UAW, the Rubber Workers, and other hard-pressed unions. His only important ally, however, was Sidney Hillman, whose Amalgamated Clothing Workers had joined the AFL only in 1934. Most union leaders viewed the CIO as another example of Lewis's self-aggrandizement.

The Goodyear conflict provided an opportunity for Lewis to show that his group could make a difference. He immediately pledged the CIO's support. Virtually all of Lewis's CIO staff visited the strike, and Adolph Germer worked closely with the strike leaders. Other CIO representatives managed the strikers' public and press relations. Although the CIO role was not decisive, it warranted the later claim that the conflict was the "first" CIO strike.

After the settlement, the Akron sit-downs continued. In the spring and summer of 1936 they became an expression of the power and independence of small groups. When the first post-strike sit-downs did not result in disciplinary action, the movement accelerated. Goodyear managers complained of more than a hundred incidents and condemned the union for failing to live up to the strike agreement. With their credibility and futures at stake, leaders of the Rubber Workers became increasingly uncomfortable. They finally prevailed upon Lewis to send his principal troubleshooter, Allan Haywood, to restore order. By the time the Flint workers occupied the Fisher Body plants, Haywood had made substantial progress in taming the sit-down movement.

The GM strike set off a similar wave of sit-downs in the auto industry and elsewhere. Although union leaders used sit-downs to win contracts at Chrysler and other firms, they were primarily expressions of rank-and-file independence, often anti-union as well as anti-employer. Union leaders were ambivalent about them. Sit-downs sustained the union's reputation for militancy but suggested a lack of control and responsibility. By the summer of 1937 a strong public backlash against sit-downs was growing. Most union leaders eventually followed Haywood's example.

By mid-1937 the problems of 1935 seemed like ancient history, and the CIO organizations, rather than the better-established unions, seemed to be "on the march." The Steel Workers Organizing Committee, headed by Lewis's right-hand man, Philip Murray, scored the coup of the decade when it won a contract from United States Steel without a strike. Union membership in the steel industry rose from a few thou-

sand to more than 100,000. Other unions also experienced unprecedented gains. Aggregate union membership rose by 1.6
million between 1936 and 1937, more than in any previous
year, with CIO unions accounting for nearly 60 percent of the
increase. Although the NLRB and other government regulatory agencies contributed, the workers themselves seemed to
be the driving force.

The collapse came with equal drama and suddenness. During the summer and fall of 1937 the economic expansion
stalled; prices and production declined and layoffs mounted,
slowly and then spectacularly. By early 1938 unemployment
was approaching the 1932–1933 level. Manufacturing again
bore the brunt of the downturn, but this time a high proportion of workers in the most vulnerable jobs were union
members. This change had two immediate and mildly contradictory effects. First, some unions were able to establish the
principle of layoffs and recalls by seniority, saving the jobs or
at least the careers of the oldest workers. Second, employers
refused to consider share-the-work plans and other measures
that might have preserved the existing labor force. Many of
them welcomed the opportunity to eliminate disloyal employees. As a result, union membership fell dramatically, particularly in the CIO organizations. The Auto, Steel, and Rubber
Workers, all dependent on the health of the auto industry,
were decimated. By the spring of 1938 the gains of 1936 and
early 1937 had evaporated.

The recession exacerbated other problems that were
equally serious. By the summer of 1937 the sit-downs and
other strikes had convinced many people outside the labor
movement that unions were more a hindrance than a help to
economic revival. The collapse of the Steel Workers' campaign to organize the Little Steel companies in June 1937 provided a chilling preview of what this perception could mean.

As the strike became increasingly disruptive and violent, elected officials in Ohio and Indiana, the principal battle-grounds, turned hostile. By the end of the conflict they were allied with the employers. As the economy declined in late 1937 and early 1938, employers and other union critics cited the recession as more evidence of the disastrous consequences of unbridled union power. Their arguments struck a respon-sive chord in many quarters. By early 1938 unions were more politically vulnerable than at any time since the 1920s.

Because of the close association between union growth and New Deal initiatives, hostility to unions became part of a widespread reaction against the Roosevelt administration and its allies. Roosevelt's ill-fated scheme to add justices to the Supreme Court, in order to achieve more favorable rulings on New Deal legislation, had alienated many supporters, and the recession raised new doubts about the recovery program and the New Deal in general. Despite all the turmoil in Washing-ton, critics argued, the economy was no better; indeed, it might be less prosperous because of New Deal regulations. In the 1938 congressional and state elections, New Deal oppo-nents, often running on explicitly anti-union platforms, won overwhelmingly. The victors, including many Southern con-servative Democrats, returned to Washington determined to end activist government and revise or repeal the most contro-versial New Deal measures. The Wagner Act was near the top of their list.

## REVIVAL AND EXPANSION, 1938–1945

The economic recovery that began in 1938 nevertheless fea-tured a modest resumption of union growth, which acceler-ated until 1944, and important changes in industrial relations. Labor-management conflict became less violent and less likely to be associated with such traditional issues as union recognition; government continued to be a decisive influence, despite its unpopularity; employers became less overtly hostile; and the public became less sympathetic to workers' complaints. The overriding reason for these developments was World War II, which profoundly altered the organizing climate.

The Supreme Court's decision in *Jones & Laughlin* (1937) was the first of a series of pro-union judgments that enabled the NLRB to enforce the provisions of the Wagner Act. As the economy revived and unions once again became active, the NLRB moved vigorously to conduct representation elections and investigate unfair labor practices. Seventy-six elections were held from October 1935 to April 1937, 890 from April to December 1937, and 2,420 from 1938 through 1940. AFL and CIO organizations won more than 75 percent of these. The election process created a new and relatively painless way to achieve recognition. It also specifically addressed one of the great hurdles of earlier years, the recalcitrant employer who refused to negotiate regardless of employee sentiment. The NLRB could not promise workers they would be covered by a contract, but it could assure them that they would not be discharged with impunity.

As a result, by the eve of World War II most industries had a significant organized sector. It often included employees of the largest, most visible firms and of smaller companies that were vulnerable to strikes. In the auto industry, for example, it encompassed almost half of all Chrysler workers, including an overwhelming majority of Detroit-area employees; about 20 percent of GM workers, including a majority in the Detroit area and in the most important component and assembly plants; and employees of many parts makers. But the persistence of the open shop at Ford, the major holdout until 1941, was a reminder that determined employers still held the upper hand. In the steel industry most United States Steel employees were union members, as were most employees of Jones & Laughlin, the other large firm that had signed a 1937 contract. Many workers at smaller specialty and supplier firms were also unionized. But Republic, Youngstown Sheet & Tube, Inland, and Armco, the Little Steel companies, remained as hostile as ever.

The following table provides a comprehensive accounting of organization in the rubber industry. By 1940 most employees of the largest firms—except Goodyear, another notable holdout—were organized. An even larger percentage of employees of medium-sized firms were union members. Most employees of small companies, on the other hand, remained unorganized. Scattered across the Midwest, New England, and, increasingly, the South, they were as hard to organize in 1940 as in earlier years.

ESTIMATES OF UNION DENSITY IN RUBBER MANUFACTURING, BY TYPE OF FIRM (PERCENTAGE OF WORKERS ORGANIZED)

| Type of Firm* | 1934 | 1937 | 1940 |
| --- | --- | --- | --- |
| Small | 7 | 14 | 15 |
| Medium | 40 | 50 | 64 |
| Large | 48 | 62 | 45 |
| All Firms | 26 | 38 | 31 |

*Small firms had fewer than 400 employees; medium firms had 400 or more employees but were single-function businesses. The large businesses (Goodyear, Firestone, B. F. Goodrich, and U.S. Rubber) were multifunction.

In this setting anti-union tactics became more sophisticated. Large corporations quickly learned to use the NLRB's own legalistic procedures to thwart organization, recognition, and especially contractual relationships. Alone or in concert with

two other measures—increased spending for employee benefit programs and encouragement of nonaffiliated labor
unions—these tactics were highly successful. As a result, anti-
unionism took two forms: the traditional, coercive approach,
common among small industrial firms and firms located in
small towns, the South, and the nonmetropolitan West, and a
more sophisticated approach common at larger, high-visibility
companies. The Ford campaign against the UAW, which depended on intimidation and coercion, was an exotic exception
to this pattern.

The story of the NLRB and of union advances in manufacturing was only part—though a highly significant part—of
the story of union activism in the late 1930s and early 1940s. In
the aftermath of the NRA, Congress passed new regulatory
measures for the transportation and energy industries designed to curb price competition, eliminate "overproduction,"
and reduce bankruptcies among producers. The 1935 Motor
Carrier Act gave the ICC oversight over highway trucking.
The 1938 Civil Aeronautics Act created a new agency, the
Civil Aeronautics Board, with similar authority over the airlines. The 1934 Federal Communications Act created a commission to regulate long-distance telephone communication
and broadcasting. Other legislation extended the jurisdiction
of the Federal Power Commission to the natural gas industry.
In each case the effect was to limit competition and introduce
government-sanctioned price-fixing. These effects in turn reduced pressures to resist union demands. Through the regulatory process, employers could pass on most of the costs of
higher wages, lower hours, and other improvements in working conditions, but they continued to bear the costs of disputes
and strikes. Regardless of their personal preferences, collective
bargaining made economic sense.

The principal beneficiary of the new regulatory environment was the Teamsters Union. Until the 1930s the Teamsters had been a union of local delivery truck and team drivers, noted for its decentralized operations and controversial associations. In Chicago, the most famous case, two Teamster organizations, a local of the International Brotherhood and an independent union, were allied with rival underworld gangs and often involved in the violent competition between them. Despite its reputation, the Teamsters had grown steadily in the 1920s as suburbanization and the growth of trucking made local transportation a growth industry. In the 1930s government regulation was an even greater stimulus. From a depression-era low of 71,000 members in 1933, the Teamsters grew to 598,000 in 1941, the largest increase of any union. It continued to grow in the following years, and in 1949 became a million-member union.

One key to Teamster expansion was the new economics of transportation; the other was the changing character of the union. From a loosely coordinated group of locals in 1930, the Teamsters became an unusual hybrid as powerful regional organizations emerged between the weak national executive and the powerful locals. The Western Conference of Teamsters, the first of the regional entities, grew out of a campaign by Seattle unionists to organize intercity truck drivers. In 1937 Dave Beck, the Seattle leader, created a single bargaining unit for thirteen Western states and British Columbia. Beck used strike threats and secondary boycotts to organize trucking companies. If organized local drivers refused to handle intercity shipments because the drivers were nonunion, the intercity companies would lose business. Since most of them were financially insecure, they usually agreed to cooperate. A Teamster contract became a prerequisite for trouble-free operations.

Beck's approach spread to other areas. In 1938 Minneapolis

organizer Farrell Dobbs created the North Central District Drivers Council (later the Central States Drivers Council) and used Beck's techniques to organize firms throughout the Midwest. Other Teamster organizers, such as James R. Hoffa of Detroit, used similar methods to expand their organizations.

In one respect, however, the Teamsters did not change. The new leaders of the 1930s and 1940s were as unscrupulous as their predecessors. Beck relied on intimidation to persuade employers to cooperate. When threats proved inadequate, he assigned thugs to emphasize the value of good relations with the Teamsters. Hoffa was even bolder. In 1939, when the CIO launched a campaign to organize truck drivers, he enlisted Detroit gangsters to attack the CIO organizers and their allies. From then on he maintained close relations with the criminal underworld. In 1940, when Teamster chiefs decided to eliminate the Minneapolis leaders who were perceived as a threat to the union because of their leftist political associations, Hoffa and a large group of "associates" temporarily moved to Minneapolis to spearhead the campaign. By then Hoffa had succeeded Dobbs as president of the Central States Drivers Council. Eliminating the Minneapolis radicals removed his only Midwestern rivals.

The growth of the Teamsters and other corrupt unions such as the International Longshoremen's Association (62,000 members by 1941), the Hotel and Restaurant Employees (260,000 by 1941), and the Hod Carriers (285,000 by 1941) exposed another side of the 1930s union revival. In industries characterized by local markets and small firms, union leaders who relied on intimidation and violence often held an advantage over employers and more scrupulous unionists. Government support for union activity supported them as well.

By 1941 government had become the most important stimulus to union growth. In addition to the Wagner Act and the regulatory measures of the late 1930s, Congress reacted to the war in Europe with far-reaching economic legislation. The repeal of the arms embargo in the fall of 1939 and the passage of Lend-Lease in the spring of 1941 opened new markets to American manufacturers. Aircraft, auto, steel, and machinery plants expanded and proliferated. By the time of Pearl Harbor, industrial production had increased dramatically, employment had grown, and labor shortages were appearing in many skilled occupations. For organizers, the economic revival created opportunities reminiscent of the mid-1930s. Aggregate union membership increased by 20 percent in 1941 and strikes, mostly for wage increases, set a record.

But a healthier economy was not the only stimulus to organization. War production was highly concentrated and wholly controlled by government. In this setting the prospect of lucrative contracts became a powerful incentive to cooperative behavior. Sidney Hillman's presence as codirector of the mobilization effort was an added reminder that government favored employers who were at peace with the labor movement. Accordingly a number of notably anti-union corporations, including Goodyear, Ford, and the Little Steel companies, agreed to collective bargaining contracts in 1941. Although many implacable union opponents remained, most employers accommodated themselves to the new reality. Their decisions reflected their assessments of the business environment rather than a change of heart or perspective.

Mobilization policy thus had an impact similar to that of the earlier regulatory measures. Neither was avowedly coercive or anti-employer. Neither explicitly addressed industrial relations issues. Yet by altering the environment, by making recognition and collective bargaining compatible with the employer's economic goals, both encouraged union growth.

The importance of the union successes before Pearl Harbor

became more apparent in the following years. During the war, government sought to promote industrial harmony and uninterrupted production by preserving the industrial relations status quo. The War Labor Board, created in early 1942, contributed a specific mechanism, maintenance-of-membership. In plants with union contracts, new employees were free to join the union; but once they did join they could not drop out and keep their jobs. Unions received the dues checkoff. They could organize nonunion plants but could not strike. As a result, union membership increased by 3.6 million between 1941 and 1945, equivalent to the entire labor movement of 1935. The vast majority of the new members were new employees of previously organized companies. The UAW was the single most important beneficiary, by 1944 doubling in size to a million members. Its largest gains were in the Big Three auto plants. By 1944 it represented virtually all Chrysler and Ford workers and a large majority of GM workers. It also acquired a large membership in farm machinery, auto parts, and aircraft manufacture, largely through employment increases.

Other major unions that doubled their membership between 1941 and 1944 included the Marine and Shipbuilding Workers (597 percent), the Food and Agricultural Workers (137 percent), the Machinists (133 percent), and the United Textile Workers (130 percent). The handful that lost membership, including the UMW, Teamsters, Hod Carriers, and Musicians, were concentrated in service industries where employment declined.

The seemingly peaceful and effortless gains of the war years nevertheless masked important challenges. As the industrial labor force grew, it also changed in potentially explosive ways. The addition of black workers created severe tensions in many war industry centers. The "hate" strikes of 1942, in Detroit and other Northern cities, and the Detroit race riot of 1943 were only the most extreme expressions of these tensions. CIO leaders in general and UAW leaders in particular responded by insisting on an inclusive approach—a reflection of their links to the UMW and the tradition of mass action, their experience with an ethnically diverse constituency, and their idealism. By 1945 the principle of racially inclusive unionism was firmly established in the industrial unions. Although many members complained in private and many AFL unions, generally those that traditionally discriminated against eastern European immigrants, remained lily-white, the labor movement made substantial progress in adapting to a changing labor force.

Despite such gains, the large membership increases of the war years had two potentially negative effects. First, they created the illusion that factory workers were no more difficult to recruit than miners, construction workers, and others. In later years organizers would complain that there were no more large factories to organize. In truth, factory workers were easy to organize only as long as government effectively restrained the opponents of organization. That restraint would soon become less effective. Second, some union leaders also may have begun to take their members for granted. The spread of the union shop, the dues checkoff, and similar union security measures, which were increasingly important features of the contractual relationships that dominated postwar industrial relations, weakened the link between union service and membership growth. Union security had never been a deterrent to union growth in mining, construction, or the services, and it probably had no immediate effect in manufacturing. But as government influence receded and employer opposition grew, it may have created an illusion of permanence. In any case, union security soon became the focus of postwar employer counterattacks.

In the immediate postwar years, union membership continued to grow until the late 1950s. Most of the growth occurred
between 1945 and 1948, as construction and manufacturing
boomed in response to pent-up consumer demand and
wartime savings, and between 1950 and 1953, the Korean War
years, when government spending and partial mobilization
created a situation reminiscent of World War II. By 1953 aggregate union membership was 36 percent higher than in
1945. In mining, construction, and transportation, unions represented three-quarters of all employees; in manufacturing,
nearly 40 percent. By most measures the postwar years were
the heyday of the labor movement, the era of Big Labor. The
economist Sumner Slichter announced the emergence of a "la-
boristic" economy.

Apart from the accuracy of such labels, no one doubted that
the rise of organized labor would have far-reaching and
durable effects. The labor movement had adapted as it had
grown; the arrival of the CIO and a new generation of executives promised decades of aggressive leadership. The Wagner
Act, the regulation of competition in many industries, and the
exigencies of the cold war similarly promised a strong government presence in the economy and industrial relations for
years to come. However reluctantly, most employers adapted
to the new order. They found, to their surprise, that collective
bargaining did not bring the dire effects they had imagined.
Indeed, despite the sweeping changes of the previous two
decades, the economy was more prosperous than it had been
since the 1920s, and the outlook was at least as favorable. And
that, perhaps, was the best indicator that organized labor was
likely to be a permanent and recognized fixture in American
economic and political life.

# 6

## The Decline of American Labor

MIDCENTURY LABOR LEADERS had good reason to be satisfied. Membership and union density were at all-time highs, and economic and political conditions seemed to favor additional growth. No one doubted that unions had become influential institutions, comparable in some respects to big business and big government. The events of the following years were therefore as unexpected as the membership surge of the mid-1930s. Unions grew in the 1950s and 1960s, though not as rapidly as the labor force; faced a series of shocks in the 1970s and early 1980s; and lost members in the 1980s and 1990s. By the early nineties union density had declined to 15 percent, scarcely better than the early thirties. Industrial unions suffered the greatest losses, but craft-industrial unions fared only marginally better. After 1975 the only unions that succeeded in attracting large numbers of new members were organizations of government employees that had little or no pre–World War II heritage. What had happened? Efforts to explain the unexpected decline of American labor typically emphasize changes in the labor force, technology, or business conditions that, it is argued, make the modern era unique. The truth is probably less melodramatic. The same factors that accounted for the rise of organized labor in earlier decades also explain its decline.

PERSPECTIVE: 1996

On July 12, 1994, the United Rubber Workers (URW) struck the Bridgestone/Firestone Company to preserve "pattern" bargaining, which had assured Firestone employees wages and working conditions comparable to those at larger and stronger competitors such as Goodyear. Several months earlier the Bridgestone managers had categorically rejected an agreement based on the Goodyear contract. Many observers believed that their real intention was to destroy the union. The ensuing conflict continued for almost twenty-seven months and exacted a substantial toll on both sides. By midsummer 1995 the union seemed to be on the verge of defeat. The Bridgestone/Firestone conflict, it appeared, would become another in a lengthening list of union setbacks. Yet the workers did not lose. The strike continued for another year and a half and resulted in a new contract that included back pay, a wage increase, and improved benefits. If less than a union victory, the agreement was surprisingly favorable. It also preserved the union at Bridgestone, no small achievement in view of the union's plight a year earlier. More intriguing was its larger meaning. If the URW's apparent demise in 1995 symbolized the problems of the labor movement, did the relatively favorable outcome of 1996 suggest a more positive future?

Bridgestone/Firestone and the URW of 1994 were remnants of powerful midcentury organizations. Firestone had been one of the best-known names in American industry for a half-century, celebrated for its shrewd marketing and high profitability. It had been the first of the large tire manufacturers to recognize the URW, in 1937, and the first to move its major production facilities from its traditional center, Akron, Ohio, to the South. Like other American tire companies, Firestone failed to keep abreast of changing technology, and in the 1970s and early 1980s it suffered substantial losses. To survive it shuttered most of its Northern factories, laid off thousands of workers, and reorganized its remaining operations. Despite its lowly state, in 1988 its managers found a buyer in Bridgestone, the leading Japanese producer, presumably for Firestone's distribution system and familiar name rather than for its factories. Firestone's continuing losses contributed to the parent company's financial decline in the years leading up to the strike.

The URW had become a formidable presence in the rubber industry because of its contractual relations with the largest firms, including Firestone. It organized virtually all the new plants these firms built between the 1940s and 1970s, though it was less successful in organizing the small, labor-intensive producers on the industry's periphery. Another problem was the union's size. Despite its influence, it never exceeded 190,000 members, a reflection of the industry's small size and its failure to recruit outside that sphere. Proposals to merge with other unions had never materialized. Meanwhile the tire makers' troubles became the union's troubles. URW membership plunged from 158,000 in 1979 to 92,000 in 1989 and 81,000 on the eve of the strike. As it declined, the URW faced more and more demands from the companies for special treatment. By the 1990s the future of pattern bargaining and the future of the union were inextricably related.

Bridgestone's response to competitive pressures and the poor performance of its Firestone subsidiary was to propose sweeping changes, including twenty-four-hour, seven-day-a-week operations and financial concessions from labor. It argued that its losses required special consideration. URW negotiators responded that the pattern concept would work in reverse: other manufacturers would demand whatever

Bridgestone received. Shortly after the strike began, the company imposed its last offer, including continuous operations. At first it operated with supervisors and salaried employees. In January 1995, however, it hired more than 2,300 strike-breakers and, with 1,000 union members who crossed the picket lines, increased production to near normal levels. Shortly afterward Local 7 in Akron, the oldest and most hallowed Firestone local, voted to return to work without a contract. Only a handful of the returning strikers were initially rehired.

During the following months the union's position continued to deteriorate. At the urging of URW leaders, President Clinton and Secretary of Labor Robert Reich publicly criticized Bridgestone/Firestone and tried to ban it from receiving government contracts. The URW also filed numerous NLRB charges against Firestone. Neither of these initiatives produced immediate results, though they publicized the dispute and tarnished the company's reputation. The union planned other protests, including demonstrations at the 1995 Indianapolis 500 auto race.

By spring 1995 the mounting costs of the strike forced URW leaders to weigh two unwelcome options. They could order the strikers back to work and admit defeat, or they could hold out, seek assistance from other unions, and hope that political pressures would ultimately have an effect. A public admission of defeat would be devastating. A recent UAW strike against the Caterpillar Company had had catastrophic effects. The UAW had struck in 1991 to enforce the industry pattern, called off the strike in April 1992, and struck again in June 1994, just weeks before the Firestone walkout. That strike would continue until December 1995 and end in another failure. The Caterpillar debacle encouraged other employers, such as Bridgestone, to be more aggressive. To

URW president Kenneth Coss, however, the lesson of the Caterpillar strike was simpler: if the mighty UAW could be humbled, what was likely to happen to the smaller and poorer URW? In March 1995 Coss began to discuss a possible merger with the United Steelworkers.

Before Coss and the union leaders could act, however, the strikers preempted them. In early May, after the NLRB dismissed some of the URW's charges against Bridgestone, members of Local 7131 in Decatur, Illinois, voted overwhelmingly to return to their jobs. Their decision was wholly unexpected. The Decatur local was supposedly the best led and most united of the striking locals. It also had strong community backing, including the support of strikers at two other major Decatur plants, including Caterpillar. Yet the local's strike fund was exhausted, a third of the members had defected, and in June the replacement workers would be able to decertify the URW. For Local 7131, the NLRB announcement was the last straw. A week later the URW called off the strike at the remaining plants and ordered union members to return to work unconditionally. Most of the returning strikers were turned away by the company and placed on a waiting list.

Contrary to most predictions, the collapse of the strike was *not* the end of the conflict. Over the next year, as the economy grew and Bridgestone recovered, most of the strikers were recalled to work. Meanwhile URW members agreed to merge with the USW in the summer of 1995, after USW leaders promised to champion the cause of the Firestone workers. In 1995 and 1996 the USW sponsored protests and demonstrations at Bridgestone facilities around the world and pressured the NLRB to punish Bridgestone. USW leaders were also among the leaders of a movement to shake up the AFL-CIO, install more vigorous leaders, and devote more resources to organizing. They cited the Caterpillar and Firestone strikes as arguments for more aggressive leadership. Their efforts succeeded in the fall of 1995 when the AFL-CIO elected a relative outsider, John Sweeney, president of the Service Employees International Union, as president. Sweeney had promised an aggressive campaign of organizing and political action.

By mid-1996 the USW's "corporate" campaign against Bridgestone/Firestone began to have an impact. Although it had no obvious effect on Bridgestone sales or profits, it promised to inspire more political attacks. And it was an embarrassment to the now prosperous company. In late October 1996, when representatives from union and management met in Chicago to discuss the union's remaining NLRB charges, Bridgestone lawyers suggested a new round of negotiations. Five days later, on November 5, an agreement was announced. Bridgestone/Firestone agreed to rehire all the strikers, pay them for work they had missed before they were recalled, raise wages across the board, and pay medical insurance premiums. The union agreed to twenty-four-hour, seven-day operations and pay incentives. The agreement, far more generous than anything the company had proposed earlier, covered 6,700 workers at seven plants. It was also compatible with the goal of pattern bargaining. USW president George Becker hailed it as a triumph.

The larger lessons of the Bridgestone/Firestone conflict were no less apparent. The struggle had demonstrated that large corporations were not invulnerable, that union resources counted, and that the economic and political environment was as influential as it had been in the 1910s or 1930s. In short, it suggested that the 1990s were not so different from earlier, happier years for unions and union members.

ORIGINS OF DECLINE

After World War II union membership did not fluctuate as it had in earlier periods. Rather than dramatic changes, aggregate membership remained comparatively stable in good times and bad. Moreover, apart from the UMW, the records of industrial unions were almost indistinguishable from those of craft-industrial organizations. Union leaders congratulated themselves on their success in overcoming the boom-and-bust cycles of the past. But there was another, less comforting side to the postwar pattern. If union membership no longer fell precipitously during recessions (it fell 2 percent during the 1948–1949 recession versus 20 percent in 1920–1922), neither did it rise dramatically in recovery periods. Aggregate membership grew 16 percent during the Korean War years (versus 95 percent between 1915 and 1920 and 70 percent between 1940 and 1945), remained virtually unchanged during the mid-1950s, and declined slightly during the 1959–1960 recession. It continued to decline during the prosperous early sixties and rose only modestly during the mid-sixties, when increased defense spending and inflation presumably should have stimulated substantial increases. Equally serious was the failure of the labor movement to grow with the economy. Although union density exceeded 30 percent between 1945 and 1958, John McBride and Peter McGuire would not have been impressed. The influence of the NLRB and other regulatory agencies, a "realistic" attitude among employers, and prosperity presumably should have opened more doors.

Why did unions fail to expand more rapidly during the prosperous postwar years? The best way to answer this question is to recall the sequence of expansion and decline common to earlier years. Union growth among autonomous workers typically led to employer counterattacks, which increased the likelihood of reprisals and made nonmembers hesitant to risk their futures. Members often had to defend their choices by striking. Contrary to contemporary opinion, this pattern was not obsolete by midcentury. Only the timing changed as government regulation discouraged the most extreme behavior and collective bargaining contracts insulated workers from some forms of intimidation. What had happened in years now took decades. The union decline that would become so evident in the 1980s had its roots in the 1940s and 1950s.

The policies of the War Labor Board between 1942 and 1945 had created severe tensions in the labor movement. WLB restraints on wages and traditional grievance procedures, which prevented workers from taking advantage of labor shortages and pressures to maximize production, were at the heart of the controversy. Union leaders were torn between their support for the war and their desire to help their constituents. John L. Lewis's insistence on exploiting wartime conditions was a warning. He succeeded in raising miners' wages but at enormous cost to the reputation of the UMW and of the labor movement as a whole. The dramatic postwar strike wave, which lasted through 1946 and set records for idle-days, created a similar paradox. Rank-and-file workers were enthusiastic beneficiaries, but unions were losers. Public revulsion against "irresponsible" and "greedy" unions that threatened postwar prosperity (at a time when many experts feared a return to depression conditions) contributed to Republican victories in 1946 and insured that the new, antiunion Congress would revive the prewar effort to curb union powers.

The resulting Taft-Hartley Act of 1947 supposedly "balanced" the powers of labor and management by subjecting unions to a variety of new restrictions. Critics argued that a genuine balance would have required a substantial increase in union power. But if the notion of "balance" was controversial, the more important point was that Congress did not simply repeal the Wagner Act, as conservatives of the late 1930s had demanded. The NLRB would continue to regulate industrial relations, though in a less partisan manner. Two factors dictated this decision. Complete deregulation would not have addressed the problem of disruptive strikes. Indeed, experience suggested that deregulation would lead to greater upheavals and violence (the postwar strikes had been notably nonviolent). In addition, employers had discovered that the Wagner Act was not as one-sided as they had originally assumed. Through legal maneuvers they had been able to thwart the pro-union character of the law and preserve the "right to manage." With a neutral NLRB they presumably would fare still better.

The anti-union potential of Taft-Hartley became apparent almost immediately in a conflict over the non-Communist affidavits that the law required union leaders to sign. Robert Denham, the new quasi-independent NLRB general counsel (another Taft-Hartley innovation), at first insisted that all union leaders, even federation officers, comply with the law. CIO officials refused, and John L. Lewis, once again a member of the AFL executive council, blocked compliance by that group. If the increasingly pro-employer Denham had had his way, the NLRB effectively would have gone out of business. Ultimately he backed down and most local and international executives signed the affidavits. The incident nevertheless showed how precarious the labor-government relationship had become in the postwar era.

In the late 1940s and 1950s the NLRB became a notable example of regulatory "capture" by powerful business groups. Typically "capture" resulted from day-to-day contacts between regulators and regulated firms. In this case the process was less subtle. President Truman's appointees, moderately prolabor, tried to satisfy both sides but only encouraged employers to intensify their attacks. Eisenhower's appointees, who dominated the board by 1954 and held all important positions by 1955, made no secret of their intention to change its direction. In 1953 congressional hearings, prominent employers had criticized the Truman appointees and proposed more acceptable policies. Their suggestions became the new board's agenda. By 1955 it had adopted all the 1953 proposals. Included were more stringent restrictions on secondary boycotts, less stringent restrictions on employer activities, and exclusion of many small businesses, including most retail firms, from NLRB jurisdiction. The Republican approach to labor law bore little resemblance to the open-shop campaign of the 1900s or the post–World War I American Plan. But its ends were similar. The Eisenhower board sought to limit regulation and make government more accommodating to employer interests. It succeeded in making life more difficult for union leaders, the future less certain for prospective union members, and the NLRB an object of partisan competition, a political "football."

If the legal and regulatory environment became less favorable to union expansion in the 1950s, the image of organized labor as the champion of the downtrodden and powerless also suffered. A series of highly publicized union scandals, involving the Teamsters and other unions with long records of unsavory activity, provided fuel for anti-union spokesmen. The effects of the Senate investigation of 1957–1958, devoted to union corruption and headed by John McClellan of Arkansas, were particularly harmful. A Gallup poll in February 1957, on the eve of the McClellan hearings, reported that 76 percent of Americans generally approved of unions. In September, after dramatic revelations about the internal affairs of the Teamsters, only 64 percent approved—the most dramatic change in twenty years of polling. Labor's approval rating never again approached the level of early 1957.

Although there was no evidence that union misbehavior had grown after World War II, the success of the labor movement in the 1930s and 1940s had made corruption a more potent issue. Union treasuries were richer, and the proliferation of insurance and pension funds created new opportunities for abuse. Infamous but small organizations, such as the International Longshoremen's Association, attracted only fleeting interest. The mighty Teamsters, which had recently passed the UAW to become the largest American union, was another matter. If the largest union could be subverted by criminals, was any union secure?

Closely related to this concern was a sense of the new role of the labor movement in society. By the 1950s organized labor insisted it was part of the American establishment, a vital force in economics and politics. The most prominent union executives, including the AFL's George Meany, who succeeded William Green in 1953, acknowledged that their organizations must meet high standards of public scrutiny. Despite the tradition of union autonomy, Meany in 1953 engineered the expulsion of the Longshoremen, the most notorious AFL affiliate. In early 1957, when he learned from McClellan Committee counsel Robert F. Kennedy that the committee had damaging evidence against Dave Beck, the Teamsters' president, he made no effort to deflect the inquiry.

Yet the most important reason for the prominence of the corruption issue in the 1950s was the McClellan Committee itself. The Kefauver and McCarthy committees of the early fifties, investigating crime and subversion, had conducted well-publicized hearings and demonstrated the ability of television to dramatize confrontations between investigators and their prey. The McClellan investigation had the same potential. One prominent committee member, Senator John F. Kennedy, hoped to use it to boost his presidential prospects. The Southern Democrats and Republicans who dominated the committee had a different goal. They hoped to discredit the labor movement and prevent Kennedy from exploiting the proceedings. The role of Kennedy's brother as committee counsel was an additional complicating factor.

Despite these diverse and contradictory interests, the needs of all factions would be served by bringing a major villain to justice. The initial focus of the committee was Beck, whose clumsy looting of the Teamsters' treasury and boorish behavior made him a convenient target. Beck was quickly exposed and convicted of misusing union funds. The committee then discovered an ever more attractive antagonist in James Hoffa, Beck's successor. Revelations of Hoffa's ruthlessness and ties to underworld groups captured headlines; his belligerent, defiant attitude created dramatic television images. The hearings proved to be only the first act in a prolonged legal contest between Hoffa and the government, but by 1958 the sordid essentials were well known. Expulsion of the Teamsters from the AFL-CIO did little to repair the damage to the labor movement.

Missing from the McClellan proceedings was any systematic exposure of the employer role in union abuses. Beck, Hoffa, and other corrupt union officials succeeded because they were allied with equally corrupt employers. Most of their misdeeds would have been impossible without accommodating allies. Indeed, the most intriguing villain exposed by the McClellan investigators was not Hoffa but Nathan Shefferman, a consultant who specialized in sabotaging unions for corporate clients such as Sears. When all else failed, Shefferman would turn to Beck and other Teamster officials for "sweetheart" contracts. His services represented a little-known dimension of the employer backlash against the Wagner Act. But these dealings were harder to explain and publicize than the excesses of union executives, and the McClellan investigators did not pursue them.

In the end nearly everyone benefited except the labor movement. Kennedy and the congressional conservatives were pleased with their headlines. Beck and Hoffa went to jail, and the public became more sensitive to union corruption. In 1959 Congress passed the Landrum-Griffin Act, which set new standards for internal union operations and tightened Taft-Hartley restrictions on union activities. Landrum-Griffin was emblematic of the hostile political climate of the 1950s. But the longer-term effects of the Teamster scandals were probably more damaging. Employers now tarred all organizers with the brush of Beck and Hoffa. Prospective union members undoubtedly thought twice about the likelihood of being robbed and bullied. The exposés had their greatest impact in the South and West, where the labor movement had only a modest base, and in the fast-growing service industries, where organization still was a relative novelty.

## EMPLOYER OFFENSIVES

Employers emerged from World War II with enhanced reputations and renewed self-confidence. Despite the unprecedented strength of the labor movement, they soon launched a campaign to contain and ultimately reverse the union gains of earlier years. Formal labor-management confrontations remained relatively placid, and strikes seldom had the winner-take-all character of earlier years. Assaults on union power more often took the form of lobbying for anti-union legislation or similar actions. Above all, employers sought to restrict unions to their postwar strongholds, a goal that proved surprisingly attainable.

While the postwar strike wave captured headlines, a CIO campaign to organize Southern industry provided a better introduction to the challenges of postwar industrial relations. Titled Operation Dixie, the CIO effort sought to recreate the aura of the great 1930s organizing campaigns. By virtually any measure, it was an overwhelming failure. Despite substantial expenditures, it attracted only a handful of members and had no appreciable influence on Southern industry. Most historical accounts of Operation Dixie emphasize flaws in the union strategy: CIO officials devoted too much attention to the textile industry, foolishly excluded radicals from their ranks, and made only halfhearted efforts to enlist black workers. Whatever the merit of these criticisms, they overlook other salient factors. CIO organizers faced staggering odds. They necessarily emphasized industries that lacked a substantial core of autonomous workers and had long traditions of anti-union activism. In these settings, employees were easily intimidated. Nor could organizers expect help from local and state governments, which were as hostile as they had been in the 1930s. The most serious union shortcomings may have been a tendency to romanticize the thirties and an unwillingness to acknowledge that determined employers, North or South, were rarely defeated.

That determination became unmistakable in the following years as business lobbyists in Southern and Western states successfully agitated for "right-to-work" laws that banned union security agreements. Right-to-work was one of many anti-union measures embraced in the 1940s by Southern legislatures; most of the others failed court challenges. Right-to-work, specifically endorsed in Section 14b of Taft-Hartley, became a way to discourage organizers and to signal that a state was probusiness. Florida and Arkansas in 1944 adopted right-to-work statutes. Within a decade nineteen other states, mostly in the South and West, adopted similar measures.

For a few years right-to-work captured the imaginations of Northern employers as well. Delaware and New Hampshire adopted right-to-work measures in the late forties, only to repeal them in the face of an aroused labor movement. The most impressive employer victory came in 1957 in Indiana. Encouraged by that breakthrough, employers' associations in Ohio and California sponsored right-to-work amendments to their state constitutions. Their campaigns galvanized union leaders and made the 1958 elections the most hotly contested of the postwar era. The result was an overwhelming defeat for right-to-work and for Republican politicians who had identified with it. Union successes reemphasized the residual strength of organized labor in the North, but they also reinforced the South's competitive edge in the interstate competition for mobile businesses. Economists' studies suggested that right-to-work laws had little direct impact on organizing. Rather, they expressed a more general hostility to organized labor which in turn accounted for the failure of most union campaigns in right-to-work states.

The limited success of right-to-work as an anti-union weapon encouraged more direct attacks on union power. The first target was the NLRB, particularly after 1961 when President Kennedy appointed Frank McCulloch, perceived as a union ally, to head the board. Employers increasingly contested board-supervised procedures, employed consultants to defeat unions in representation elections, and appealed NLRB rulings. In many cases they also sought to create a climate of intimidation through discharges and warnings of layoffs, plant closings, and other adverse effects of union contracts.

Although many of these tactics were illegal, the penalties, if any, were so puny that they had little deterrent effect. Union victories in representation elections declined from more than 80 percent in the 1940s to less than 50 percent in the 1970s. At the same time business groups launched a spirited public relations campaign against the McCulloch NLRB. Liberally financed by large corporations, the campaign sought to revise the law to reverse prolabor rulings and end the board's legal responsibility to encourage collective bargaining. Despite Richard Nixon's victory in 1968, Democratic control of Congress thwarted the legislative effort. Nixon appointees to the board gradually reversed some of McCulloch's rulings but had little taste for thoroughgoing change.

These public activities gradually changed the meaning of government regulation, but they probably had less impact than parallel developments in industry. Although small and medium-sized firms often resorted to aggressive union avoidance measures, big businesses were able to deter organization in more subtle ways. Technological innovation and increasing foreign competition, particularly after the mid-1960s, provided powerful stimuli to cost-reducing innovations. To many corporate managers, the easiest way to reduce costs was to relocate operations to small towns and rural areas of the South and West. Union avoidance was rarely the dominant motive; but a nonunion labor force was insurance that the other advantages of these areas, such as low wages, would persist. Anti-unionism thus combined with more general concerns about operating costs to stimulate a sweeping decentralization of industry.

This process occurred over several decades and attracted little attention. Unlike the employer response to Operation Dixie, the shift in large-scale manufacturing was notably undramatic. Until the 1970s it rarely featured plant closings. In older plants, managers and union leaders continued to resolve grievances, negotiate contracts, and confront each other in "civilized" strikes. At the same time their companies opened new plants, usually in semirural Southern settings. Union organizers typically found the new employees reluctant to pay dues to an organization that might jeopardize their futures. Companies rarely opposed union representation directly, and there were few confrontations. Yet in the course of a decade or more, the proportion of production employees who were union members fell. Equally important, organized employees found themselves increasingly isolated in older plants that, because of high costs, received little attention or investment. By 1970 union members in many industries were precariously exposed.

This pattern, which differed in detail from firm to firm, was also associated with broader changes in corporate operations that also had anti-union implications. One of these was the growth of technical and professional employment and government regulations, which necessitated a personnel staff devoted to "human resources" rather than to union relations and collective bargaining. Human resources managers had little personal stake in collective bargaining; indeed, they typically viewed it as an historical artifact. They also championed work reorganization in order to involve employees in shop-floor decision-making and improve morale. Since union leaders opposed changes that were likely to reduce their influence, experimental techniques were more likely to be introduced in nonunion plants, further distinguishing between organized and unorganized facilities. The other major change in corporate policy, which became apparent only in the 1970s, was the growing power of line managers, whose preoccupation with production and suspicions of staff managers (including industrial relations *and* human resources managers) was consistent

with a trend toward smaller, more isolated plants and less bu-
reaucracy.

How did unions respond to these changes? The record is
varied, but many did surprisingly little, either because of complacency or fatalism. Some union officials delayed action as
long as their treasury was solvent and the rank and file did not
rebel. A larger number were political pragmatists; their constituents were current members who expected attention and
services, not unorganized workers hundreds of miles away.
Without an overt threat, it was difficult to justify the diversion
of scarce resources to risky organizing campaigns. When business challenged them directly, as in 1958, they responded aggressively and effectively. In quieter times they defended the
status quo. Organizing expenditures fell rapidly between the
1950s and 1980s, along with the number of NLRB elections.

Industrial unions faced the most serious challenges. By the
1950s the United Steelworkers had become a lethargic giant.
The UAW supported a variety of social causes and insistently
followed the auto makers south. Yet it too failed to extend its
reach. Other industrial unions had similar experiences. The
major exception to this pattern of complacent stability was the
UMW, which in the 1950s entered another near-fatal down-
ward spiral. The coal industry's problems became more severe
after World War II as consumption declined and competition
intensified. In the late 1940s Lewis negotiated a series of innovative contracts. In 1950, however, he entered into a covert
partnership with George Love, the leading coal employer. In
return for approving draconian layoffs that ultimately cost the
jobs of most UMW members, and, in the historian Curtis
Seltzer's words, becoming "the Bituminous Coal Operators
Association's thug, doing its dirty work in the name of his
members," Lewis enjoyed a prosperous, secure old age. Un-

like other union leaders, Lewis and his cohorts made no effort
to defend the status quo.

Another apparent reason for the decline in union organizing was the 1954–1955 AFL-CIO merger. Beset by poor leadership and chaotic organization, the CIO declined rapidly
after World War II. Apart from a half-dozen large unions like
the Steel and Auto Workers, its affiliated unions were small
and poor; most were not even self-supporting. Some AFL officials urged George Meany to let the CIO collapse. Meany,
however, thought a merger would be less disruptive. Given
this background, it is not surprising that the merger failed to
stimulate a new era of union activism. The no-raiding pact
that preceded the merger reduced competition for members
and became an excuse to devote even fewer resources to organizing.

Clearly by the late 1960s the labor movement faced a formidable list of problems. Yet it is important not to read the disasters of later years into this period. Organized labor was still
larger and stronger than at any time before World War II.
Aggregate membership was at record levels, and though
union density had declined, union defenders could argue that
the growth of white-collar unionism would soon reverse that
trend. If that *had* happened, the 1950s and 1960s might be
compared to the 1920s. But all the problems of the fifties and
sixties became more severe in the seventies, marking that
decade as the beginning of an era with no obvious historical
antecedent.


## COLLAPSE

The decade from 1973 to 1982 was devastating for union
and nonunion workers alike. The energy crises of 1973–1974

and 1979–1980, and the severe recessions they precipitated, were only the most obvious signs of trouble. Rising energy costs spurred attacks on inflation and a national consensus that lower prices resulting from competition were preferable to industry stability. The resulting deregulation movement undermined the intricate business-labor partnerships that had characterized the transportation, energy, and communications industries. The dislocations of the 1970s also exposed problems that had accumulated during the easy prosperity of the postwar era. Growing competition decimated firms that had long been viewed (and viewed themselves) as world leaders. Yet the collapse of the seventies and early eighties paved the way for new opportunities. The economy revived, technological innovation accelerated, and employment grew rapidly—with a notable exception. American unions did not revive with the economy; indeed, after 1983 organization continued to decline in most industries.

The pattern of decline was unmistakable. In the fifties and sixties membership had grown slightly, though density had decreased. In the seventies membership stagnated and density declined to little more than one-fifth of the nonagricultural labor force. The severe recession of the early 1980s eliminated more than 2 million union members, far more than any previous postwar recession, and the following decade saw additional losses. The following table compares union density by industry in 1983 and 1994. During that decade aggregate union membership fell by 6 percent. If public-sector unions had not added almost 1.5 million new members, the loss would have been almost 14 percent. By 1994 only 10.8 percent of private-sector employees were union members. The typical worker of the 1990s was no more likely to be a union member than his or her grandparents or great-grandparents of the 1910s.

UNION DENSITY, 1983, 1994 (PERCENTAGE)

| Industry | 1983 | 1994 |
|---|---|---|
| Mining | 20.7 | 15.6 |
| Construction | 27.5 | 18.8 |
| Manufacturing | 27.8 | 18.2 |
| Transportation | 42.4 | 28.4 |
| Trade | 8.7 | 6.2 |
| Finance | 2.9 | 2.3 |
| Services | 7.7 | 6.2 |
| Government | 36.7 | 38.7 |
| All Industries | 20.1 | 15.5 |

Initially union losses were the result of adverse economic developments largely unrelated to industrial relations. The dramatic decline of the steel, auto, and auto components industries in the 1970s and the emergence of the Midwestern "rust belt" devastated the Steelworkers, Auto Workers, Rubber Workers, and other unions of industrial workers. The fate of the tire industry was representative of the larger phenomenon.

American tire companies had been slow to embrace the radial tire, which, among other things, enhanced automobile fuel efficiency. The energy crisis of 1973–1974 transformed the tire market, creating opportunities for Michelin and other foreign companies that specialized in radials. Facing catastrophic losses, American tire manufacturers had little choice but to shift to radial production. They did have a choice, however, about where they made radial tires. They could reorganize their Northern plants, install new machinery, and retrain veteran workers, or they could expand their Southern operations, some of which were nonunion, and hire new workers.

Meanwhile contract negotiations between the manufacturers and the URW stalled in 1976 over the union's demand for automatic cost-of-living adjustments. The result was a bitter nationwide strike that lasted four months. Together with a long history of labor-management friction, the strike strongly reinforced the manufacturers' inclination to favor their newer Southern factories. The second energy crisis and the recession of the early 1980s sealed the fate of the Northern plants. By 1986 the tire companies had closed thirty-two plants, including their oldest and largest factories, and eliminated thousands of union jobs. Firestone closed all its older plants but still was unable to close the gap with its competitors.

The campaign to deregulate industry, another result of the economic crisis of the 1970s, had similar effects on unions in transportation and communications. The deregulation of airlines, railroads, and trucking between 1977 and 1980 created new cost pressures in a period of economic decline. Many well-established airline and trucking companies merged or went out of business; new companies were less receptive to worker demands; nonunion firms proliferated. Union losses in transportation were proportionately as great as in manufacturing, though the precise impact varied widely. In the airline industry, for example, employees whose jobs were industry-specific, such as pilots and flight attendants, saw their wages plummet by as much as two-thirds. Others, like mechanics, whose skills were easily transferrable to other industries, successfully resisted wage and benefit concessions. In trucking, unionized, high-cost companies that provided generic services suffered the greatest losses. The survivors demanded wage and benefit concessions or created nonunion subsidiaries. Nonunion, low-wage firms such as J. B. Hunt captured most of the truckload business. In the 1980s average drivers' wages fell by more than one-quarter. The workers' plight cost the

Teamsters more than a quarter-million members and accelerated efforts to reform the union.

The breakup of AT&T in 1983–1984 had similar effects on
telephone workers. More than 300,000 AT&T employees lost
their jobs between 1983 and 1994, with the Western Electric
manufacturing division hardest hit. The company had been 67
percent organized before the breakup; by the early nineties it
was 46 percent organized. New telephone competitors, notably MCI and Sprint, were aggressively anti-union.

The long-term effects of these developments were equally
threatening to unions. The economy revived after 1982, but
price competition remained a potent influence on employer
behavior. The cost-cutting experiences of the recession years
also alerted employers to the possibilities of boosting short-
term profits by cutting jobs and wages or moving production
south or to low-wage countries such as Mexico. Probably the
most important long-term effects, however, were political.
The economic turmoil of the 1970s created opportunities for
conservative politicians whose policies left little or no role for
organized labor.

The fate of a union-sponsored labor reform bill in
1977–1978 was a harbinger of political change. After many
years of fruitless attacks on Section 14b, the right-to-work
provision of Taft-Hartley, the AFL-CIO adopted a more realistic strategy, promoting a bill to streamline NLRB procedures
and encourage organization. In 1977 the House of Representatives passed it overwhelmingly. But in 1978, when the Senate considered the bill, business interests launched an all-out
campaign against it. Despite Democratic control of the Senate,
the bill failed. Senators from states with large concentrations
of union members had supported it, regardless of party. But
by the late 1970s there were not enough highly organized
states to assure passage. The election of Ronald Reagan two

years later, over strong union opposition, was a logical sequel to the battle over the reform bill.

The Reagan administration was notably hostile to regulatory measures in general and to collective bargaining and union activism in particular. Reagan's discharge of striking air traffic controllers in 1981 signaled this hostility. His frequent criticism of union behavior also tacitly encouraged anti-union activity. But his most important initiative was a deliberate and largely successful effort to complete the transformation of the NLRB into a pro-employer agency. In 1983 he named Donald Dotson, an attorney with close ties to anti-union groups, as board chairman. Together with other Reagan appointees, Dotson reversed many NLRB policies and precedents. The Dotson board excluded many economic issues from collective bargaining and turned representation elections into no-holds-barred contests for employee loyalty. By the late 1980s the NLRB did not even give lip service to the goal of encouraging collective bargaining. Instead it provided a veneer of legality for traditional open-shop policies. In an apparent reversal of the pattern that dated from Section 7a of the NIRA, government effectively discouraged organization.

Employers, including firms that had had collective bargaining contracts for decades, began to weigh the possibilities of eliminating unions from their older plants. The result was a series of bitter strikes—the best known at Phelps-Dodge in southern Arizona in 1983–1984, Hormel in Austin, Minnesota, in 1985–1986, Caterpillar in 1991–1995, and, finally, Bridgestone/Firestone in 1994–1996. Each of these companies faced severe competitive pressures and a well-established union. When the unions rejected demands for concessions and struck, the companies hired replacement workers and tried to operate nonunion facilities. Despite enormous costs, they were victorious—or so it seemed. Union members either lost their jobs, crossed the picket line, or returned as individuals after the strike ended. Their plight symbolized the vulnerability of even the most powerful unions. Only the surprising conclusion to the Bridgestone/Firestone conflict suggested that unions might break the pattern of defeat and decline.

The combined effects of deregulation, industrial decentralization, and employer and government hostility created a strongly hostile environment and a decline in organizing, as union membership data indicate. A defensive union establishment, unwilling to devote resources to organizing, exacerbated these problems. Yet there was an intriguing exception to this pattern. Government employees, who had been an insignificant factor in the labor movement of the 1930s and 1940s, became a large and growing force in the labor movement of the 1980s and 1990s. Their activism was the most positive feature of the union experience of those years.

### REBIRTH?

After 1960 workers in the burgeoning service industries accounted for most union membership gains and a rapidly increasing share of the labor movement as a whole. The majority of white-collar union members were government employees (see the table on page 151). Their growing prominence and the prominence of their organizations (by the 1990s the National Education Association and the American Federation of State, County, and Municipal Employees were larger than the Teamsters, nearly twice as large as the UAW, and more than three times as large as the Carpenters) raised important questions about the future of the labor movement. Would miners and factory workers be replaced by police officers, teachers, janitors, and bureaucrats? Or was the growth of public-employee unions a harbinger of other changes, comparable to the growth of artisans' and miners' unions in the mid-nineteenth century?

The growth of public-employee organizations seemingly resolved one important issue: white-collar work per se posed no obstacle to organization. Many statistical studies of union membership associated the post-1960 decline with broader economic changes that increased service-sector employment. But that association was misleading, reflecting the historically low level of service-sector organization rather than the inclinations of contemporary service-sector workers. If mid-nineteenth-century artisans had conducted similar studies, they probably would have concluded that the growth of rail transportation and factory production limited their potential. They would have been correct in the sense that economic change restricted the potential of the existing labor movement, but wrong in the larger and more relevant sense. The failure of many unions of the 1960s and 1970s to adapt to changing economic opportunities probably depressed membership growth at that time. But their shortcomings did not foreclose the possibility of future growth, as the experiences of the minority that did adapt (or were favorably situated from the beginning) amply suggest.

Like the miners, railroad workers, and highly skilled factory workers who became the core of the late-nineteenth- and early-twentieth-century labor movement, service-sector workers often have substantial workplace autonomy. Even if they are subject to rigid schedules, have to meet arbitrary quotas, or are poorly paid, they typically have considerable leeway in planning their work, organizing materials, and allotting their time. Most of them are expected to spend a minimum number of hours each day at their jobs, but they usually are not supervised like factory workers. They are probably best compared to traditional miners or construction workers.

Many of them also have a strong consciousness of their occupations. The more highly skilled have professional associations that regulate entry to the profession and perform other economic functions. The history of the National Education Association, transformed from a sleepy professional organization into the nation's largest union in a decade, underlines the potential of such groups.

A critical consideration for service-sector workers is the likelihood of reprisals. In many professions, dismissal from one's job is tantamount to dismissal from the profession. Public-sector workers typically have protection against arbitrary discharge, and the courts increasingly have extended similar rights to private-sector workers. But less extreme and more subtle reprisals are possible. The marked difference in the level of organization between private and public college faculties (5 percent versus 37 percent in the mid-1980s, for example) is largely a result of the Supreme Court's 1980 *Yeshiva* decision, which excluded private college faculty members from NLRB jurisdiction. As a result, faculty members who favor collective bargaining must confront school administrators and the risks that such encounters entail. Even if they have tenure, they remain vulnerable to other forms of reprisal, such as lower salary increments and less desirable teaching schedules.

The single most successful organizing story of the post–World War II era, the emergence of professional athletes' unions, is also a commentary on the relationship between such threats and worker behavior. Until the middle of the twentieth century, team owners wholly controlled the (usually brief) careers of their players. They could trade them to another team or fire them without explanation or appeal. Although basketball, baseball, football, and hockey players formed associations between 1953 and 1957, the players' organizations initially had little economic impact. The Major League Baseball Players Association, spurred by its more prominent and secure members, became the catalyst for change. In 1966 it hired an aggressive executive secretary, a longtime union activist and negotiator, and became a de facto union. The impact was apparent almost immediately. A formal collective bargaining contract, signed in 1968, created an institutional structure. Amid much turmoil, including a strike in 1972 and a lockout in 1976, the players won more generous pensions and higher minimum salaries, which pleased the marginal players, together with free agency and salary arbitration, which benefited the stars. By 1976 the other three major professional sports also had collective bargaining agreements. The process and results were similar. Once a handful of star players had demonstrated their willingness to defy the owners, the other players joined them to monopolize the labor force and take advantage of the growing national appetite for spectator sports.

For most service-sector workers the prospect of reprisals remains a serious threat and a potent influence. Although many employers do not participate in anti-union business associations, their hostility to collective bargaining is no less vigorous than that of traditional industrial managers. Relatively new companies like Walmart and MCI, which have grown rapidly by undercutting competitors' prices, are especially hostile. In this setting, two political factors largely dictated the pattern of organization in service occupations. The first was the anti-establishment protests of the sixties and early seventies that made workers conscious of the possibilities of addressing grievances through mass action and collective bargaining. The second was the passage of public-employee bargaining laws that formally reduced the resistance of public-sector employers to union activity.

A notable characteristic of the growth of white-collar unionism was its timing. Before 1960 there was relatively little activity. An upsurge of activism and dramatic union gains in the sixties and early seventies was followed by another period of relative inactivity and modest union losses, roughly the late seventies to mid-eighties. Until the late seventies this pattern did not coincide with the larger pattern of union activity or seem to be influenced by it. Indeed, case studies suggest that workers were far more responsive to societal developments than to the activities of unions or the policies of the AFL-CIO. The single most important stimulus was probably the civil rights movement, which had a direct and immediate impact on black workers and an indirect but no less important effect on others. Civil rights agitation seemingly demonstrated the efficacy of organization at a time when the Teamster scandals, Landrum-Griffin, and the apparent complacency of AFL-CIO leaders had raised doubts of the value of organization for rank-and-file workers.

A prime example was the growth of Local 1199 of the Retail Drug Employees Union. After many years of indifferent success as a union of New York City pharmacy employees, it began to organize hospital workers. From the beginning Local 1199 organizers targeted low-wage, low-skill employees. Despite this apparent handicap, they were able to draw on the example of the civil rights movement to build an aggressive constituency and keep hospital administrators on the defensive. The local's first hospital contract came in late 1958, its first large strike in mid-1959. As it expanded, it enlisted the city and state AFL-CIO organizations in a successful campaign to win nonprofit hospital workers collective bargaining rights under state law. What had begun as a rebellion of dissatisfied workers, comparing themselves to victims of racial segregation, became a more conventional organizing cam-

paign which succeeded in the comparatively liberal environment of the Northeast. By 1970 Local 1199 had thirty thousand members, including three-quarters of New York City's
hospital employees.

New York's municipal employees unions had similar experiences. AFSCME District Council 37 started as a union of
park laborers, expanded rapidly in the 1960s, in part by identi-
fying with the civil rights movement, and became a major
force in New York local government. The teachers' successes
were equally impressive. In the 1930s teachers' unions had had
a large New York membership but in the forties and early
fifties had lost most of their following. In the late fifties, however, the American Federation of Teachers affiliate took advantage of male teachers' dissatisfaction with their relatively
low pay to enlist a corps of activists. It conducted a short, successful strike in late 1960, defeated the local NEA affiliate in a
representation election in 1961, and in February 1962 conducted another short strike. The following September it concluded a collective bargaining contract with the school board.
These victories enhanced the union's reputation and publicized its objectives. In the following years the AFT negotiated
contracts with school boards in other large cities.

Equally important was the impact of this activity on teachers in suburban and small-city systems. Encouraged by the example of the big cities, they became more restive and more
critical of the narrow focus of the NEA. By the late 1960s they
had forced NEA leaders to embrace collective bargaining,
which spread rapidly. In effect there were now two powerful
teachers' unions. Merger talks between the AFT and NEA in
the 1970s broke down over such issues as the organization of
nonteaching employees and affiliation with the AFL-CIO.
Because of its huge base, the NEA remained about four times
as large as the AFT. The more important point, however, was

that public school teaching (and public college teaching to a lesser degree) had been transformed as dramatically as public service employment in large cities.

The relationship between these events and the passage of public-employee bargaining laws has provoked much controversy. Were the laws causes or results of union activism? Initially, as these examples indicate, unions and bargaining laws were *both* products of heightened public sensitivity to injustice and discrimination. Government employees saw themselves as victims of neglect and indifference, and, like other aggrieved groups, relied on mass action and political pressure to agitate for change. Success in one area or by one occupational group inspired workers in other areas and occupations. Meanwhile five states adopted public employee bargaining laws in the 1960s; nineteen, including virtually all the highly urbanized states, passed bargaining laws in the next decade. The laws in turn marked the beginning of a second, more deliberate phase of union activity. Whereas teachers often organized and negotiated collective bargaining contracts without state assistance, police and firefighters made little progress until legislatures acted. Bargaining laws typically banned strikes by safety workers and created procedures for arbitrating disputes, eliminating the most serious—and traditionally paralyzing objections—to collective bargaining. The other notable effect of legislation was to circumscribe the employers' range of permissible anti-union tactics. As long as unions remained politically active, the law seemingly precluded vigorous anti-union activity.

The parallel between these developments and the events of the 1930s and 1940s is obvious. Government activism galvanized and directed public unrest in 1933 and 1934, helped break down the distinction between autonomous workers and others, and indirectly encouraged the spread of mass organizing methods. The decisions of the NLRB and the War Labor Board built on these initiatives. Similarly the worker protests of the early sixties created a foundation for public-sector union growth in the seventies and eighties.

Although unions have achieved additional gains among public employees in the 1990s, they have had less success in recruiting service-sector workers generally. As a result, the distinction between private and public employment has become more marked. Does the labor movement have a future in the private sector of the economy? The experiences of the past century and a half suggest that a substantial revival is likely, though its timing and dimensions are impossible to predict. The growing number of jobs with shop-floor autonomy is a positive sign, as is the strength of public-employee unions and the spread of favorable state legislation (despite the plight of the NLRB). Aggressive union avoidance activities, by emphasizing the possibilities of a collective voice, may, ironically, have a similar effect. Future historians are likely to view the growth of white-collar unions in the 1960s and 1970s much as we view the rise of the American Miners Association in the 1860s and the railroad brotherhoods in the 1870s—the first halting steps in the rise of a movement that flourished for a century and profoundly affected the lives of members and nonmembers alike.

Thus the factors that shaped the labor movement over the last century and a half are likely to have a substantial effect on its future. They include the role of autonomous workers, who have typically dominated the labor movement; employer policies, which have always been influential, often decisive; and the larger economic and political environment, which has been a powerful influence, especially in determining the timing of union growth and decline. The interaction of these forces over time largely explains the ebb and flow of the American labor movement. That fact is also the most important reason for believing that the dramatic membership decline of recent decades will be only the latest chapter in an ongoing, unpredictable, and continually fascinating drama.

# A Note on Sources

THE LITERATURE of American labor is vast. The following notes identify major sources and provide suggestions for additional reading and study.

### 1: UNION GROWTH IN PERSPECTIVE

Of the many works that address the issues of union growth and decline, the following provide useful introductions from a variety of perspectives: Richard Freeman and James Medoff, *What Do Unions Do?* (New York, 1984); Michael Goldfield, *The Decline of Organized Labor in the United States* (Chicago, 1987); Barry T. Hirsch and John T. Addison, *The Economic Analysis of Unions: New Approaches and Evidence* (Boston, 1986). The classic article on the role of the autonomous worker is Benson Soffer, "A Theory of Trade Union Development: The Role of the 'Autonomous Workman,'" *Labor History* 1 (Spring 1960), 141–163.

Estimates of union density are based on the following sources: John R. Commons, *et al.*, *History of Labour in the United States*, vol. I (New York, 1918), 424; Stanley Lebergott, *Manpower in Economic Growth: The American Record Since 1800* (New York, 1964), p. 510; David Montgomery, *Beyond Equality: Labor and the Radical Republicans, 1862–1872* (New York, 1967), p. 140; Norman J. Ware, *The Labor Movement in the United States, 1860–1895: A Study in Democracy* (New York, 1929), p. 66; Leo Troy, *Trade Union Membership, 1897–1962* (New York, 1965), p. 2; U.S. Bureau of Labor Statistics, *Handbook of Labor Statistics, Bulletin 2070* (December 1980), p. 412; Michael Curme, Barry T. Hirsch, and David A. Macpherson, "Union Membership and Contract Coverage in the United States, 1983–1988," *Industrial and Labor Relations Review* 44 (October 1990), 9; U.S. Department of Commerce, *Statistical Abstract of the United States, 1995* (Washington, D.C., 1995), p. 445.

## 2: MINERS AND ORGANIZED LABOR

The quotation in the introductory paragraph is from Andrew Roy, *A History of the Coal Miners of the United States* (1905, reprinted Westport, Conn., 1970), p. 70. Roy's comment on labor migration after the Civil War is from p. 105; on conflicts between miners' unions at the end of the chapter, from p. 264. The story of the 1894 strike is based on news reports that appeared in the *Chicago Tribune*. Also see the relevant chapters in Richard Jensen, *The Winning of the Midwest: Social and Political Conflict, 1888–1896* (Chicago, 1971), and Paul Kleppner, *The Cross of Culture: A Social Analysis of Midwestern Politics, 1850–1900* (New York, 1970). John McBride is a sadly neglected figure. Michael Pierce's essay, "The Making of the Populist President of the American Federation of Labor: The Political Transformation of John McBride, 1880–1894" (forthcoming, *Labor History*), is a corrective.

Useful works on the coal industry and coal miners include Katherine A. Harvey, *The Best-Dressed Miners: Life and Labor in the Maryland Coal Region, 1835–1910* (Ithaca, N.Y., 1969); Harold W. Aurand, *From the Molly Maguires to the United Mine Workers: The Social Ecology of an Industrial Union, 1869–1897* (Philadelphia, 1971); Perry K. Blatz, *Democratic Miners, Work and Labor Relations in the Anthracite Coal Industry, 1875–1925* (Albany, N.Y., 1994); David Brody, "Market Unionism in America: The Case of Coal," *In Labor's Cause: Main Themes in the History of the American Worker* (New York, 1993); Chris Evans, *History of United Mine Workers of America,* 2 vols. (n.p., n.d.); Ronald L. Lewis, *Black Coal Miners in America: Race, Class, and Community Conflict, 1780–1980* (Lexington, Ky., 1987); Anthony F. C. Wallace, *St. Clair: A Nineteenth-Century Coal Town's Experience with a Dis-*

*aster-Prone Industry* (New York, 1987); and Edward Wieck, *The American Miner's Association: A Record of the Origin of Coal Miners Unions in the United States* (New York, 1940).

Comparable studies of hard-rock mining and miners' unions include Ronald C. Brown, *Hard-Rock Miners: The Intermountain West, 1860–1920* (College Station, Tex., 1979); David M. Emmons, *The Butte Irish: Class and Ethnicity in an American Mining Town, 1875–1925* (Urbana, Ill., 1989); Vernon H. Jensen, *Heritage of Conflict: Labor Relations in the Nonferrous Metals Industry up to 1930* (Ithaca, N.Y., 1950); Larry Lankton, *Cradle to Grave: Life, Work, and Death at the Lake Superior Copper Mines* (New York, 1991); Richard E. Lingenfelter, *The Hardrock Miners: A History of the Mining Labor Movement in the American West, 1863–1893* (Berkeley, 1974); Philip J. Mellinger, *Race and Labor in Western Copper: The Fight for Equality, 1896–1918* (Tucson, 1995); Mark Wyman, *Hard Rock Epic* (n.p., n.d.); and Joseph H. Cash, *Working the Homestake* (Ames, Ia., 1973). Cash's statement regarding the Homestake union is from p. 40.

## 3: URBAN WORKERS AND ORGANIZED LABOR

The story of the Burlington strike is based on Donald L. McMurry, *The Great Burlington Strike of 1888: A Case Study in Labor Relations* (Cambridge, Mass., 1956); C. H. Salmons, *The Burlington Strike* (1889, reprinted New York, 1970); and Reed C. Richardson, *The Locomotive Engineer, 1863–1963: A Century of Railway Labor Relations and Work Rules* (Ann Arbor, 1963).

John R. Commons, *et al., History of Labour in the United States* (New York, 1918), the first two volumes of the four-volume study, is the classic account of the growth of organized labor in the nineteenth century. The quotation is from I, 7–8. Other useful volumes include Bruce Laurie, *Artisans into Workers: Labor in Nineteenth-Century America* (New York, 1989); Sean Wilentz, *Chants Democratic: New York City and the Rise of the American Working Class, 1788–1850* (New York, 1984); Richard Stott,

*Workers in the Metropolis: Class, Ethnicity, and Youth in Antebellum New York City* (Ithaca, N.Y., 1990); Cynthia J. Shelton, *The Mills of Manayunk: Industrialization and Social Conflict in the Philadelphia Region, 1787–1837* (Baltimore, 1986); Thomas Dublin, *Women at Work: The Transformation of Work and Community in Lowell, Massachusetts, 1826–1860* (New York, 1970); and Alan Dawley, *Class and Community: The Industrial Revolution in Lynn* (Cambridge, Mass., 1976). Peter Temin, *The Jacksonian Economy* (New York, 1969) examines the inflation issue.

For the Civil War era, see David Montgomery, *Beyond Equality: Labor and the Radical Republicans, 1862–1872* (New York, 1967). A good case study is Frank T. Stockton, *The International Molders Union of North America* (Baltimore, 1921).

Norman J. Ware's *The Labor Movement in the United States, 1860–1890: A Study in Democracy* (New York, 1929) has held up remarkably well. The quotation regarding national unions is from p. 1; regarding the Knights of Labor from p. 61. Other important works on the labor movement of the 1880s include Kim Voss, *The Making of American Exceptionalism: The Knights of Labor and Class Formation in the Nineteenth Century* (Ithaca, N.Y., 1993); Richard Jules Oestreicher, *Solidarity and Fragmentation: Working People and Class Consciousness in Detroit, 1875–1900* (Urbana, Ill., 1986); Mary H. Blewett, *Men, Women, and Work: Class, Gender, and Protest in the New England Shoe Industry, 1780–1910* (Urbana, Ill., 1988); Melvyn Dubofsky and Warren Van Tine, *Labor Leaders in America* (Urbana, Ill., 1987) (chapters by Montgomery on William Sylvis, John H. M. Laslett on Samuel Gompers, and Oestreicher on Terence V. Powderly); Melton Alonza McLaurin, *The Knights of Labor in the South* (Westport, Conn., 1978); and Leon Fink, *Workingmen's Democracy: The Knights of Labor and American Politics* (Urbana, Ill., 1982). The Oestreicher quotation is from p. 115. For late-nineteenth-century unions, see Lloyd Ulman, *The Rise of the National Trade Union* (Cambridge, Mass., 1955); Robert Christie, *Empire in Wood: A History of the Carpenters' Union* (Ithaca, N.Y.,

1956); Paul Krause, *The Battle for Homestead, 1880–1892: Politics, Culture, and Steel* (Pittsburgh, 1992); Stuart Bruce Kaufman, *Samuel Gompers and the Origins of the American Federation of Labor, 1848–1876* (Westport, Conn., 1973); John T. Cumbler, *Working-Class Community in Industrial America: Work, Leisure, and Struggle in Two Industrial Cities, 1880–1930* (Westport, Conn., 1973); and Dorothee Schneider, *Trade Unions and Community: The German Working Class in New York City, 1870–1900* (Urbana, Ill., 1994).

Knights of Labor statistics are from Daniel Nelson, *Managers and Workers: Origins of the Twentieth-Century Factory System in the United States, 1880–1920* (Madison, Wisc., 1995), p. 123, and adapted from Voss, *The Making of American Exceptionalism*, p. 124.


## 4: New Environments, New Challenges

The story of the 1922 shop craft strike is based on the accounts in Robert K. Murray, *The Harding Era: Warren G. Harding and His Administration* (Minneapolis, 1969); Colin J. Davis, "Bitter Conflict: The 1922 Shopmen's Strike," *Labor History* 33 (Fall 1992), 433–455; and Robert H. Zieger, *Republicans and Labor, 1919–1929* (Lexington, Ky., 1969).

The miners' history can be traced in Blatz, *Democratic Miners*; Evans, *UMW*, vol. 2; Craig Phelan, *Divided Loyalties: The Public and Private Life of Labor Leader John Mitchell* (Albany, N.Y., 1994); Lewis, *Black Coal Miners*, and Price V. Fishback, *Soft Coal, Hard Choice: The Economic Welfare of Bituminous Coal Miners, 1890–1930* (New York, 1992). The fate of the WFM is ably described in Melvyn Dubofsky, *We Shall Be All: A History of the Industrial Workers of the World* (Chicago, 1969) and Vernon Jensen, *Heritage of Conflict* (Ithaca, N.Y., 1950). The best source on the Colorado war is George Suggs, Jr., *Colorado's War on Militant Unionism: James H. Peabody and the Western Federation of Miners* (Detroit, 1972). For the Michigan campaign, see Arthur W.

Thurner, *Rebels on the Range: The Michigan Copper Miners' Strike of 1913–1914* (Lake Linden, Mich., 1984). James Foster's study is entitled "An Inquiry into the Fall of the WFM and Summary of the WFM Codebook," in Foster, ed., *American Labor in the Southwest: The First One Hundred Years* (Tucson, 1982), pp. 33–45. The quotation is from p. 40. For the West Virginia campaigns, see David Alan Corkin, *Life, Work, and Religion in the Coal Fields: The Southern West Virginia Miners, 1880–1920* (Urbana, Ill., 1981), and Lon Savage, *Thunder in the Mountains: The West Virginia Mine War, 1920–21* (Pittsburgh, 1990). Also helpful is J. W. Hess, ed., *Struggle in the Coal Fields: The Autobiography of Fred Mooney* (Morgantown, W. Va., 1967). The Colorado Fuel & Iron strike is the subject of George S. McGovern and Leonard F. Guttridge, *The Great Coalfield War* (Boston, 1972) and H. M. Gitelman, *Legacy of the Ludlow Massacre: A Chapter in American Industrial Relations* (Philadelphia, 1988). The casualty figure is from Philip Taft and Philip Ross, "American Labor Violence: Its Causes, Character, and Outcomes," in Hugh Davis Graham and Ted Robert Gurr, eds., *Violence in America: Historical and Comparative Perspectives* (New York, 1969), p. 332.

The union resurgence is described in Selig Perlman and Philip Taft, *History of Labour in the United States, 1896–1932*, vol. 3 (New York, 1935). Membership statistics are from Wolman's *Ebb and Flow*. Also see the relevant sections of Christie, *Empire in Wood*; David Brody, *Steelworkers in America* (Cambridge, Mass., 1960), and Michael Kazin, *Barons of Labor: The San Francisco Building Trades and Union Power in the Progressive Era* (Urbana, Ill., 1987). The Glocker quotation is from "Amalgamation of Related Trades in American Unions," *American Economic Review* 5 (September 1915), 554. Also see the early chapters of Christopher Tomlins, *The State and the Unions: Labor Relations, Law, and the Organized Labor Movement in America, 1880–1960* (Cambridge, Mass., 1985). For the open-shop movement, see Perlman, *History of Labour*; Sidney Fine, *"Without Blare of Trumpets": Walter Drew, the National Erectors' Association and the Open Shop Move-*

*ment, 1903–57* (Ann Arbor, 1995); Daniel R. Ernst, *Lawyers Against Labor: From Individual Rights to Corporate Liberalism* (Urbana, Ill., 1995); and the relevant sections of David Montgomery, *The Fall of the House of Labor: The Workplace, the State, and American Labor Activism, 1865–1925* (New York, 1987).

The IWW strikes are examined in Dubofsky, *We Shall Be All*; Anne Huber Tripp, *The IWW and the Paterson Silk Strike of 1913* (Urbana, Ill., 1987); John Ingham, "A Strike in the Progressive Era: McKees Rocks, 1909," *Pennsylvania Magazine of History* 90 (July 1966), 355–376; and Daniel Nelson, *American Rubber Workers and Organized Labor, 1900–1941* (Princeton, 1988). For the clothing workers' strikes, see Melvyn Dubofsky, *When Workers Organize: New York City in the Progressive Era* (Amherst, Mass., 1968); and Steve Fraser, *Labor Will Rule: Sidney Hillman and the Rise of American Labor* (New York, 1991).

For World War I, see the appropriate chapters of Montgomery, *Fall of the House of Labor*; Brody, *Steelworkers in America*; Brody, *The Butcher Workmen* (Cambridge, Mass., 1964); David Goldberg, *A Tale of Three Cities: Labor Organization and Protest in Paterson, Passaic and Lawrence, 1916–1921* (New Brunswick. N.J., 1989); Brody, *Labor in Crisis: The Steel Strike of 1919* (Philadelphia, 1965); and Dubofsky, *We Shall Be All*. Government intervention is addressed in Melvyn Dubofsky, *The State and Labor in Modern America* (Chapel Hill, 1994); Valerie Jean Conner, *The National War Labor Board: Stability, Social Justice, and the Voluntary State in World War I* (Chapel Hill, 1983); and Austin Kerr, *American Railroad Politics, 1914–1920: Rates, Wages, and Efficiency* (Pittsburgh, 1968).

Useful sources for the 1920s include Irving Bernstein, *The Lean Years: A History of the American Worker, 1920–1933* (Cambridge, Mass., 1960); Zieger, *Republicans and Labor*; and Melvyn Dubofsky and Warren Van Tine, *John L. Lewis, A Biography* (Urbana, Ill., 1986).

Union membership growth is from Wolman, *Ebb and Flow in Trade Unionism*, 172–192.

## 5: THE LABOR MOVEMENT AT HIGH TIDE

The story of the General Motors strike is based on Sidney Fine's magisterial *Sit-Down: The General Motors Strike of 1936–37* (Ann Arbor, 1969), still the best work on the labor upheavals of the mid-1930s. For the earlier and later sit-down movements, see Nelson, *American Rubber Workers*, and Fine, *Frank Murphy: The New Deal Years* (Chicago, 1979).

New Deal policy is traced in Ellis Hawley, *The New Deal and the Problem of Monopoly: A Study in Economic Ambivalence* (Princeton, 1966); Dubofsky, *Labor and the State*; James Gross, *The Making of the National Labor Relations Board: A Study in Economics, Politics, and the Law* (Albany, N.Y., 1974); and Gross, *The Reshaping of the National Labor Relations Board: National Labor Policy in Transition, 1937–1947* (Albany, N.Y., 1981).

The union response to Section 7A has been studied extensively. Irving Bernstein, *Turbulent Years: A History of the American Worker, 1933–1941* (1970) is the best-known survey. The UMW is covered in Dubofsky and Van Tine, *Lewis*; the UAW in Sidney Fine, *The Automobile Under the Blue Eagle: Labor, Management, and the Automobile Manufacturing Code* (Ann Arbor, 1963); the clothing industry in Fraser, *Hillman*; the rubber industry in Nelson, *American Rubber Workers*; the New York transit industry in Joshua Freeman, *In Transit: The Transport Workers Union in New York City, 1933–1966* (New York, 1989); the West Coast longshoring industry in Bruce Nelson, *Workers on the Waterfront: Seamen, Longshoremen, and Unionism in the 1930s* (Urbana, Ill., 1988).

The anti-union backlash of the late 1930s is examined in Bernstein, *Turbulent Years*, and Fine, *Murphy*. For the attacks on the NLRB, see Gross, *Reshaping of the NLRB*, and Tomlins, *The State and the Unions*.

The principal source on the CIO in the 1930s and 1940s is Robert Zieger, *The CIO, 1935–1955* (Chapel Hill, 1995). AFL unions have received less attention. For the Teamsters, see Donald Garnel, *The Rise of Teamster Power in the West* (Berkeley,

1972) and Arthur A. Sloane, *Hoffa* (Cambridge, Mass., 1991); for the purge of the Minneapolis Teamsters, see Thomas L. Pahl, "G-String Conspiracy, Political Reprisal, or Armed Revolt? The Minneapolis Trotskyite Trial," *Labor History* 8 (Winter 1967), 30–52.

All the union histories mentioned above examine the impact of World War II on membership. Of particular importance are Zieger, *CIO*, and Nelson Lichtenstein, *The Most Dangerous Man in Detroit: Walter Reuther and the Fate of American Labor* (New York, 1995). I have traced the remarkable growth of the UAW in "How the UAW Grew," *Labor History* 35 (Winter 1994), 5–24. Also see August Meier and Elliott Rudwick, *Black Detroit and the Rise of the UAW* (New York, 1979). Postwar conflicts and tensions are described in detail in Stephen Meyer, *"Stalin Over Wisconsin": The Making and Unmaking of Militant Unionism, 1900–1950* (New Brunswick, N.J., 1992).

Estimates of union density in rubber manufacturing are from Daniel Nelson, "Managers and Non-Union Workers in the Rubber Industry, Union Avoidance Strategies in the 1930s," *Industrial and Labor Relations Review* 43 (October 1989), 43.


6: The Decline of American Labor

The story of the Bridgestone/Firestone strike is based on newspaper accounts in the *Wall Street Journal*, *New York Times*, and *Akron Beacon Journal* between 1992 and 1996.

The effects of War Labor Board policies are examined in Nelson Lichtenstein, *Labor's War at Home* (New York, 1982). The postwar history of the NLRB is the subject of James Gross's important book, *Broken Promise: The Subversion of U.S. Labor Relations Policy, 1947–1994* (Philadelphia, 1995). Howell John Harris, *The Right to Manage: Industrial Relations Policies of American Business in the 1940s* (Madison, Wisc., 1982) covers the immediate postwar era. The Teamster scandals and the McClellan investigation are addressed in Sloane's *Hoffa* and R. Alton Lee, *Eisen-*

*hower and Landrum-Griffin: A Study in Labor-Management Politics* (Lexington, Ky., 1990). George Meany's role is described in Joseph Goulden, *Meany* (New York, 1972) and in Archie Robinson, *George Meany and His Times: A Biography* (New York, 1981). The public opinion data is from Seymour Martin Lipset and William Schneider, *The Confidence Gap: Business, Labor and Government in the Public Mind* (New York, 1983).

For employer union avoidance strategies, see Elizabeth A. Fones-Wolf, *Selling Free Enterprise: The Business Assault on Labor and Liberalism, 1945–60* (Urbana, Ill., 1994) and Sanford Jacoby, "Employee Attitude Testing at Sears, Roebuck and Company, 1938–1960," *Business History Review* 60 (Winter 1986), 602–632. The defeat of Operation Dixie is detailed in Zieger, *CIO*, and in Barbara S. Griffith, *The Crisis of American Labor: Operation Dixie and the Defeat of the CIO* (Philadelphia, 1988). The best historical source on right-to-work is Gilbert J. Gall, *The Politics of Right to Work: The Labor Federations as Special Interests, 1943–1979* (New York, 1988). For the economic effects, see Hirsch and Addison, *Economic Analysis of Unions*. For the NLRB in the 1950s and 1960s, see Gross, *Broken Promise*. The rise of nonunion systems is the subject of Thomas A. Kochan, Harry C. Katz, and Robert McKersie, *The Transformation of Industrial Relations* (New York, 1986).

For union approaches to collective bargaining, see Chapter 5 in David Brody, *Workers in Industrial America: Essays on the 20th-Century Struggle* (New York, 1980), together with the case studies in the following: Gerald G. Somers, ed., *Collective Bargaining: Contemporary American Experience* (Madison, Wisc., 1980); David B. Lipsky and Clifford B. Donn, *Collective Bargaining in American Industry: Contemporary Perspectives and Future Directions* (Lexington, Mass., 1987); and Paula B. Voos, *Contemporary Collective Bargaining in the Private Sector* (Madison, Wisc., 1994). Labor's social activism is addressed in Kevin Boyle, *The UAW and the Heyday of American Liberalism, 1945–1968* (Ithaca, N.Y., 1995). For Lewis's postwar stewardship of the UMW, see Dubofsky and Van Tine, *Lewis*; Brody, "Market Unionism," *In Labor's Cause*; and Curtis Seltzer, *Fire in the Hole: Miners and Managers in the American Coal Industry* (Lexington, Ky., 1985). The quotation is from p. 82. For the AFL-CIO merger, see Zieger, *CIO*, and Goulden, *Meany*.

The case studies noted above include important information on the crises of the 1970s and early 1980s. In addition, see Peter Cappelli, "Competitive Pressures and Labor Relations in the Airline Industry," *Industrial Relations* 24 (Fall 1985), 316–338; Pierre-Yves Cremieux, "The Effects of Deregulation on Employee Earnings: Pilots, Flight Attendants, and Mechanics, 1959–1992," *Industrial and Labor Relations Review* 49 (January 1996), 223–242, and Michael H. Belzer, "Collective Bargaining After Deregulation: Do the Teamsters Still Count?" *Industrial and Labor Relations Review* 48 (July 1995), 636–655. The problems of the tire industry are addressed in Mark D. Karper, "Tires," in Lipsky and Donn, *Collective Bargaining*, pp. 79–101; Charles Jeszeck, "Structural Change in CB: The U.S. Tire Industry," *Industrial Relations* 25 (Fall 1986), 229–247; Jeszeck, "The Decline of Tire Manufacturing in Akron," in Charles Craypo and Bruce Nissen, eds., *Grand Designs: The Impact of Corporate Strategies on Workers, Unions, and Communities* (Ithaca, N.Y., 1993), pp. 18–44; and Thomas A. Kochan, Robert B. McKersie, and Peter Cappelli, "Strategic Choice and Industrial Relations Theory," *Industrial Relations* 23 (Winter 1984), 16–39. Gross, *Broken Promise*, discusses the fate of labor reforms and the NLRB in the 1980s. Jonathan D. Rosenblum, *Copper Crucible: How the Arizona Miners' Strike of 1983 Recast Labor Management Relations in America* (Ithaca, N.Y., 1995) and Dave Hage and Paul Klanda, *No Retreat, No Surrender: Labor's War at Hormel* (New York, 1989) examine major strikes.

Important case studies of service-sector unionism are included in Somers, *Collective Bargaining* (especially Robert E. Doherty, "Public Education," pp. 508–535) and Lipsky and Donn, *Collective Bargaining in American Industry* (James B. Dworkin, "Professional Sports," pp. 187–223; Samuel B. Bacharach, Timothy P. Schmidle, and Scott C. Bauer, "Higher Education," pp. 225–264; John Thomas Delaney and Peter Feuille, "Police," pp. 265–306). Also see Richard B. Freeman and Casey Ichniowski, eds., *When Public Sector Workers Unionize* (Chicago, 1988) and Benjamin Aaron, Joyce M. Wajita, and James L. Stern, *Public Sector Bargaining*, 2nd ed. (Washington, D.C., 1988). Leon Fink and Brian Greenberg, *Upheaval in the Quiet Zone: A History of Hospital Workers Union, Local 1199* (Urbana, Ill., 1989) traces the evolution of an important union. Mark H. Maier, *City Unions: Managing Discontent in New York City* (New Brunswick, N.J., 1987) examines other New York City unions. Ruth Milkman, "Union Responses to Workforce Feminization in the United States," in Jane Jenson and Rianne Mahon, eds., *The Challenge of Restructuring: North American Labor Movements Respond* (Philadelphia, 1993), pp. 226–250, discusses the roles of women in unions.

Union density figures are from U.S. Department of Commerce, *Statistical Abstract of the United States, 1995* (Washington, D.C., 1995), p. 445.

# Index

## A NOTE ON THE AUTHOR

Daniel Nelson is professor of history at the University of Akron. Born in Indianapolis, he studied at Ohio Wesleyan University and Ohio State University, and received a Ph.D. in American history from the University of Wisconsin. He specializes in labor and business history, and has also written *Managers and Workers, Farm and Factory, Unemployment Insurance, Frederick W. Taylor and the Rise of Scientific Management, American Rubber Workers and Organized Labor*, and *A Mental Revolution*.